HOW TO MAKE FRIENDS EASILY

Discover How To Talk To Anyone And Make New Friends,
No Matter What Age You Are

REBECCA COLLINS

D1521960

The content contained within this book may not be reproduced, duplicated or transmitted without direct written permission from the author or the publisher.

Under no circumstances will any blame or legal responsibility be held against the publisher, or author, for any damages, reparation, or monetary loss due to the information contained within this book. Either directly or indirectly. You are responsible for your own choices, actions, and results.

Disclaimer Notice:

Please note the information contained within this document is for educational and entertainment purposes only. All effort has been executed to present accurate, up to date, and reliable, complete information. No warranties of any kind are declared or implied. Readers acknowledge that the author is not engaging in the rendering of legal, financial, medical or professional advice. The content within this book has been derived from various sources. Please consult a licensed professional before attempting any techniques outlined in this book.

By reading this document, the reader agrees that under no circumstances is the author responsible for any losses, direct or indirect, which are incurred as a result of the use of the information contained within this document, including, but not limited to, — errors, omissions, or inaccuracies.

Copyright Notice

All rights reserved.

No part of this book may be reproduced in any form or by any electronic or mechanical means, including information storage and retrieval systems, without written permission from the author, except for the use of brief quotations in a book review.

Under no circumstances will any blame or legal responsibility be held against the publisher, or author, for any damages, reparation, or monetary loss due to the information contained within this book. Either directly or indirectly. You are responsible for your own choices, actions, and results.

FTC Disclosure, some links in this book may be affiliate links. This means that the Author/Publisher will receive some compensation in the form of commission from the sale of the product.

Enjoy the book.

CONTENTS

INTRODUCTION

"I have no friends."

That was the truth, not too many years ago.

What with trying to get my career off the ground and raising a young family, my life was way too busy for anything else.

I was completely absorbed in the daily routine of getting the kids to daycare, rushing to the office, and attending back-to-back meetings before running back home to do dinner and the 'goodnights'.

It was quite a gruelling period in my life as I tried to juggle several roles: mum, wife, homemaker, and businesswoman. My hubby also had a demanding career and we hardly spent any quality time together as a family or as a couple, for that matter.

But, I felt Ok. I was actively pursuing my dreams and had two adorable children and a loving partner. What else could I possibly need?

The truth is, that I didn't allow myself to address the fact that I had no friends at that time. Sure, I had colleagues, family, neighbors, and associates, but no one that I could turn to for a good chat or rely on when I was having a meltdown.

Despite being in daily contact with so many people, it wasn't until I overheard a conversation at my regular zumba class that I realized just how friend-less I was.

I've always been quite independent, and never thought twice about going somewhere alone if I needed to. I'd been attending zumba regularly for about three months and the classes were usually packed with about 30 or so enthusiastic participants. They all seemed to know each other and were always chatting away and laughing throughout the session, while I never struck up a conversation with anyone. I must have seemed very antisocial looking back, but no one ever tried to talk to me either.

As I was getting ready to leave after one particular evening class, I overheard the other women arranging to meet up together afterward at a local pizza place. I felt a tinge of envy.

On the way home, it dawned on me that, although going to the class alone was no big deal, it would have been so much more fun if I had also felt a part of the group.

As for pizza night, I clearly wasn't invited and why would I be? I never said more than a 'Hi' to anyone or made any effort to get to know my fellow zumba fans better. In truth, it hit me that I had forgotten how to make friends.

But it isn't just about zumba and pizza. Having friends means so much more than that. They can be your mentors, confidantes, and supporters. They will pick you up when you are down, lend a trusted ear to share your problems with, and bring greater joy into your life.

They will be there when you need them, have your back, and always be honest with you. Who wouldn't like some of that?

I did have close friends when I was younger but since moving to a new city, I had lost touch with most of them over time. Once I became aware of how much I missed having people in my life who I could call friends, I started to look at what I had been doing wrong.

The answer to that is, nothing. I had simply put having friends low on my list of priorities, thinking that I could do without them. That bad habit gradually left me feeling lonely, but I couldn't see it. It wasn't until the 'pizza' conversation that I had to admit it – I had no friends.

I'm sure that many of you might be experiencing the same thing and would like to change that. You could be living in a totally different place to where you grew up and find it difficult to keep up with old friends or meet new ones there.

Perhaps you are leading a very busy life, with hardly any free time to yourself. In the moments you do have to relax, you may have little energy to make an effort to socialize. That's perfectly OK and I can understand why you would feel that way.

It may even be that you are shy or on the introverted side and don't feel comfortable starting a conversation with someone you don't know. Even if you are in regular contact with people at work, college, or the gym, you may find it difficult to open up and prefer to avoid engaging in any kind of conversation.

In a world where 'friends' are very often online or 'virtual' and not people we have ever met, it could be that we have become lazy about our friend-making skills.

I don't think you can compare having 563 Facebook friends to having a few genuine connections with people who actually know you and love you in real life, despite all of your flaws. Having said that, engaging with friends on social media is better than nothing, but it can't replace real face-to-face contact.

After talking to other people in my role as mentor, I get the impression that many of them actually feel isolated but don't know how to break through that wall of getting to know someone better. They aren't sure what to say, worry that they will be viewed negatively, and feel awkward about appearing 'too friendly'.

We don't want to appear creepy or desperate, right?

It's a lot easier to keep to yourself than to open up to another person. Why expose your inner thoughts or feelings to someone who may not understand you, or be reliable and trustworthy? It's certainly safer to maintain your distance and use social media as your main form of interaction.

After all, there's no obligation on your part to show up, be honest, or reveal your true self. You don't have to commit to anything. Sure, not all digital connections stay that way and you will have heard of cases where people actually meet up and become good friends, even romantic partners. But for the most part, we seem to be forming 'fake friendships' rather than real friends.

My belief is that we do want to have friends and understand the need, but we are so out of practice. We've forgotten how to interact and hold a conversation face-to-face that doesn't involve emojis. In addition to that, we aren't that willing to invest the time and energy needed to form more meaningful bonds.

The fallout of this is that more and more of us find ourselves feeling totally alone, emotionally stunted, and socially isolated. The longer we feel that way, the less likely we are to brave the real world and start making friends. Was it always this way?

There are differing opinions about that but all the recent studies show that many of us find it more and more difficult to strike up a simple conversation with someone, never mind build a genuine friendship. Yes, the hardest part about making friends seems to be talking to someone in the first place.

You aren't the only one in this boat. In fact, a recent study by an app called Patook found that about 70% of those who participated said they had difficulty making friends. Women seem to have an even harder time, as do young adults, and moving from one city to another seems to play a large role too. Whether it's linked to your age, gender, location, or life-style, you need to do something to get out of the 'no friends' trap.

That's why I decided to write this book because I would like to help you to learn how to make real friends, no matter what your situation.

Most of you probably had childhood friends and didn't have to think about the problem until later on in life. Kids are very social animals and can bond extremely quickly with their peers.

Spending a large part of their day with hundreds of other kids of the same age means that school is the perfect way to forge lifelong friendships. You may have friends from kindergarten that you are in touch with even today, and are much more likely to retain those close bonds if you both still live in the same town or location.

It's when we enter the real, adult world that things start to get difficult, such as starting university or beginning your first job. Now, you have to start from scratch, finding people you get along with or have similar interests with. That's by no means easy.

Maybe you needed to move away from home to an area where you knew absolutely no one, which can be tough. Naturally, it takes some time to adjust and fit in, and we aren't always prepared to handle that. After all, none of us are taught the social skills needed to strike up conversations with perfect strangers.

As a society, we are even encouraged to avoid that, because we don't want to come across as rude, nosey, or intrusive.

It could be that you have suffered a bad experience with a close friend who you feel let you down, leaving you with certain trust issues that have prevented you from forging new friendships. If you were betrayed by someone you relied on or confided in, it's not easy to get over that and the fear of making the same 'mistake' again is a problem.

It's even possible that you suffer from a lack of confidence or low self-esteem and don't believe that you have anything interesting to bring to the table. If you have a negative impression of yourself, it's extremely difficult to overcome that and feel you are worthy of someone's attention.

As a stay-at-home-mum or dad, the likely scenario is that you don't have much opportunity to mix with other adults, which can mean that making new friends is almost impossible. You probably feel exhausted a lot of the time as you put your children's needs before that of your own and don't have any social life anymore.

If you are one of the new generation of remote workers, although working from home has a lot of perks, there is a downside to that. You probably have less real interaction with the outside world, only connecting with people over ten minute Zoom chats.

Opportunities to create any meaningful relationships are reduced and if you don't push yourself to get out more, you may eventually get used to this self-imposed isolation.

These are all valid explanations of why you now find yourself without friends, but it doesn't mean that things have to stay that way. There are plenty of practical strategies that you can learn to form genuine friendships whatever your circumstances and the benefits can be truly life-changing. Let me put it this way:

- **What if you could gain the confidence to approach potential friends and be able to develop a fulfilling relationship with them?**

- **How about learning ways to open up to people and allowing them to get to know you better and actually like you?**

- **If the thought of making small talk sounds terrifying, what if you could develop strategies for overcoming those fears?**

- **Wouldn't it be wonderful to learn how to make new friends easily at school, college or in a totally new city?**

- **How about finding ways to look forward to holiday seasons like Christmas, instead of dreading them because you have no one to share them with?**

- **By getting to know all about something called the Pareto Principle and learning how to use it,**

maybe you can unlock the door to new, long-lasting friendships.

I'm going to cover all of the above in this book, but don't expect me to simply tell you to join a club or get out more, because we all know that it's not how this works.

The art of making friends has more to do with how we feel about ourselves than about where we go, what we do, or who we meet. Like I said earlier, I was a career-driven, happily married mum who came into contact with many people every day, but still found myself lacking any close friends.

What was I doing wrong, and how did I make it right? That's what you are going to discover in the following pages.

We'll begin by looking at why having friends is so important and what benefits they can bring into our lives. It may seem obvious, but having friends plays a vital role in our mental and physical well-being, apart from the companionship they provide. If that wasn't the case, we wouldn't feel so bad about not having any in the first place.

If you would like to discover how to make new friends or explore ways to help your young/teenage kids to develop their friend-making skills, you will find a lot of practical help in this book. It does require some effort and a genuine desire to open up to others, but I think you are ready for that.

All you need to do now is come with me as we set off on a friend-finding mission like no other.

Be brave. Be positive. And be yourself. That's the most important step of all!

Free for you.

10 Weekly Issues of Rebecca's life-changing newsletter "Reclaim Your Power" Rebecca covers Self Love, Self Esteem, Making Friends, Getting Your Life Back & Living A Life of Freedom.

https://rebecca.subscribemenow.com/

WHY FRIENDS ARE SO IMPORTANT

A friend is a gift you give yourself.

— *Robert Louis Stevenson*

You can't fully comprehend just how important friends are until you find yourself without them.

Friends serve profound needs that just can't be met by family, colleagues, or acquaintances. Although it's difficult to describe exactly what a friend is as it may mean different things to different people, everyone likes to have them. With friends, life is simply nicer, richer, and more rewarding.

Quite frankly, you are missing out on so much in life without friends. Apart from having someone to hang out with or a shoulder to cry on, the emotional bonds that are created between friends are truly unique and can last a lifetime. In fact, no other relationship can bring you the same level of unwavering loyalty, self-enrichment, and honesty.

You may have sisters, brothers, a spouse, partner, or work colleagues, but none of these are necessarily going to be good friends. They can be, but that's not always the case.

Family ties are something different from friendship and although most people love their siblings or relatives, they don't always classify them as good friends. As the well-known saying goes, 'you can choose your friends but you can't choose your family'.

Our relatives are connected to us through biology and although we can't change that, we can decide if we actually like them or not, often feeling closer to a friend than to a sister or brother.

Partners or spouses can also be great friends and many people profess that their husband/wife/partner is also their best friend. That's great until the relationship breaks down, which often means losing both a friend and partner in one fell swoop. Relying on a partner to meet all of your emotional needs could leave you without a social circle outside of the relationship, which can be a bad thing in the long run.

The people you work with can also be your friends, although your relationship may be strictly work-oriented and never extend into a more social setting. If you or they leave the job, or the dynamic of your working relationship shifts, that can be the litmus test for how strong your friendship really is.

We can have friends from all realms of our lives, but what makes those relationships special is the deep platonic connection that we have with each other rather than any biological, romantic, or work-related ties.

Friendship is really a gift that you give to yourself because it is the one thing that brings absolute joy. It's the icing on the cake, the laughter through the sadness, and the light in the darkness.

Having someone to depend on who will be there for you no matter what, and who will always be truthful, even if that hurts, is invaluable.

Friends also serve a much more practical purpose because having them can improve your mental health and physical well-being, leading to a longer life. That may sound a bit far-fetched but it happens to be true.

If you have a strong social support system, you are much less likely to suffer from health issues like depression, high blood pressure, and obesity. Ask any octogenarian what the key to a long life is and apart from the usual 'staying healthy and active', they will also mention, 'having good friends'.

The benefits of having besties are multiple and below you will find some of the reasons why building strong friendships can seriously improve your life.

State of Mind. Having friends can literally keep you balanced. They will help to put your problems into perspective and stop you from obsessing about how bad your day was. By taking your mind off any negative thoughts, you can refocus on other things and have a laugh rather than feel sorry for yourself. You may wake up in the worst of moods but after spending time with friends, the world looks wonderful again.

Mental Health. Most people suffering from depression describe feeling lonely or isolated. Although these feelings don't necessarily cause depression, they can play a part if prolonged.

While some of us can manage being alone for a certain duration of time without a significant effect on our mental health there are those who desperately crave companionship. Having friends would certainly make them feel better about life as a whole and reduce the risk of depression.

Physical Well-being. Loneliness increases the amount of cortisol in the brain, which is the stress hormone. It's also responsible for a healthy immune system which, if left vulner-

3

able, can lead to diabetes, sleep disorders, heart problems, and even cancer. Even if you don't meet up with friends often, just knowing that they are there if you need them helps to control the amount of stress that you may experience.

Sharing is Caring. A problem shared is a problem halved, as they say, and this definitely applies to friendships. Negative thoughts, worries, and concerns can eat away at you but if you have someone to share them with, it is literally like taking a weight off your shoulders.

It's not feasible to deal with problems on your own all of the time, and having an understanding friend by your side is certainly very useful.

A Support System. Whenever you go through a difficult phase in your life, as we all do, having someone to support you can make all the difference.

Just talking to someone who passes no judgment and acknowledges how you feel can be very empowering. And while you may be way too hard on yourself, a true friend will show you kindness and help you to get back on track.

Keeping Active. A life without friends probably means too much time spent in front of the TV, the computer screen, or your mobile phone. Having friends makes you more active as you take part in outdoor events, go walking, play sports, or plan other activities together. This is vital for your physical health, as well as being much more fun than sitting at home alone.

De-stressing. It's important to relieve stress and spending time with friends can do that. Even a phone call or a five-minute chat may be all it takes to help you get to a better headspace.

You can have a moan about your job or the kids, and immediately feel better afterward. Bottling everything up inside you is a surefire way to accrue large amounts of harmful stress for body and soul.

Talking Sense. One other advantage to having friends is that they will often talk more sense than we do when we feel emotionally charged. Their level-headedness can save us from acting without thinking and making serious mistakes.

They help us to calm down when we cannot do it ourselves, acting as a stop valve for irrational or destructive behavior.

Adding Meaning. We are all capable of going to a football match alone, but it's so much more fun when we share the experience. Spending your leisure time with friends brings more value to each moment and gives your life extra purpose and meaning. This is essential for a healthy mindset, even if your favorite team loses!

Having a Confidante. Being able to share your deepest thoughts, emotions, and even secrets can be very liberating. Friends offer a space where you can express yourself, safe in the knowledge that your confidence won't be breached.

Trust and loyalty are essential in any relationship but in a friendship, they are a crucial prerequisite and without them, the pact will inevitably break down.

Being Honest. We need people to be honest with us, even if it doesn't feel too pleasant at the time. A good friend will tell you the truth, no matter how much it is going to hurt, because they have your best interests at heart in the long run.

If your partner is cheating on you, or your new outfit looks awful, wouldn't you rather hear it from a friend than from a stranger?

Personal Encouragement. Good friends will help you to achieve your goals by giving you constant encouragement. When you find yourself losing hope or becoming disillusioned, they will be the ones to spur you on to the finish line.

Friends will be there to congratulate you when you reach the end and even if you fail, they will coax you into reaching for new goals and dreams.

Self-Development. Making friends and maintaining those friendships needs a lot of give and take on both sides. It can be a learning process in which we grow and mature, coming to terms with our faults and allowing ourselves to improve and be a better person.

Through friendships, we also acquire better social skills and learn how to communicate more effectively with those around us.

Being Yourself. When you are with friends, you don't feel the need to be anyone other than who you truly are. This allows you to be free of social restraints and criticism, where you can speak your mind and express your opinions openly.

True friends will like you no matter what you think or believe, even if they don't agree with you. They have also seen you at your best and your worst and still like you, warts and all!

Unconditional Love. They say that man's best friend is a dog because it loves its owner unconditionally, and they are probably right. If you can form friendships with people who love you without expecting anything back in return, then you have discovered the secret to what a true friend is.

You may be loved by your family, which is great, but the unconditional love of a friend isn't linked to blood ties or from any sense of responsibility. It is pure, unadulterated friendship.

Enjoyment. Friends help you to enjoy life more. Together, you can do fun activities, laugh, joke, and spend time doing the things you both love. This is an essential bonding experience that contributes to forming lifetime friendships with fond memories as their foundations.

Laughter is also extremely good for you and letting your hair down now and again is the best kind of therapy there is.

Quality of Life. Having friends increases your sense of belonging and combats feelings of social isolation and loneliness. You may have few or no family members, and therefore, friends can often be a genuine substitute and kindred spirit.

They will also help you to deal with trauma, pain, loss, and illness, providing you the support that you need to deal with all of the challenges in life.

It's all about having real connections with people that you like who, in turn, like you. This is a mutual bond that knows no limits. I often think of Christopher Robin and Winnie The Pooh - two fictional characters created by A.A. Milne, who depicts the beauty of friendship so well in his books.

Both boy and bear would pass the day conversing about what being friends means, exchanging wisdom that still carries great weight today. Quotes such as, *"A day without a friend is like a pot without a single drop of honey left inside,"* reveal just how bitter the absence of a friend can be in our lives.

Friends come in all shapes and sizes and friendships can be struck up between the most unsuspecting people. Some of the most well-known friendships in history were between figures you wouldn't normally put together. Mark Twain and Helen Keller, T.S Eliot and Groucho Marx, Ella Fitzgerald and Marilyn Monroe spring to mind.

But there are also lots of fictional besties from pop culture who we love because of their undying devotion to each other and unconditional love.

We have Thelma and Louise, Bill and Ted, Frodo and Sam, and even Shaggy and Scooby-Doo. Great friendships, wherever they come from, stand the test of time and we love these characters because we understand what they give to each other – the gift of friendship.

Maybe that's one of the reasons why the popular American sitcom 'Friends' was such a big hit. It allowed us, the audience, to take part in the lives of a group of good friends and experience all of their ups and downs from the safety of our homes.

It was fun, entertaining, had some great characters, and covered life's problems so well.

Why seek real friends when we have Joey or Rachel to rely on, right? The appeal of 'Friends' is evident even today, with 20-somethings rediscovering a world of old-fashioned nostalgia free of Twitter and Tiktok references. The beauty and power of the show lay in its portrayal of genuine, platonic love, which is something that many of us seem to be missing today.

It's very common for young children to have 'imaginary friends'. In fact, up to 65% of children below the age of 7 are reported to have had an imaginary companion, making it pretty normal behavior.

My eldest son had an invisible friend until about the age of 4, which seemed strange at first but we got used to it. We had to set an extra dinner plate for his 'friend', and leave an empty chair for him to sit on. When my second son came along and reached the toddler stage, my eldest son now had a real person to amuse himself with and his invisible friend eventually stopped showing up for dinner.

What does this phenomenon tell us about the basic human desire to have friends? Maybe quite a lot, with researchers mentioning things such as meeting a child's need for support, companionship, and entertainment.

As parents, we can provide all three but having friends to do that just seems to be much more fun.

You don't need to have hundreds of friends —quality is obviously better than quantity. Even if you have a long list of people you know, having one or two people who you can count on through thick and thin is more meaningful than lots of 'superficial' acquaintances.

Nurturing such close friendships takes time and effort, so you must be prepared to do so as we go through this book.

As I mentioned in the Introduction, I'm not going to tell you that you need to go out today and start hunting today for the perfect friend. What I will tell you instead is that you can find friends anywhere, anytime.

There will always be opportunities to make new friends, no matter at what stage of your life you find yourself in. But before you can do that, you need to begin by asking yourself one crucial question: **what kind of friend can I be?**

That's the most important step you need to take because if you don't know how to be a good friend, how can you expect to find one?

Let's explore ways to do exactly that in the next chapter!

Key Points:

- *No other relationship can offer you the same merits as true friendship.*

- *Friends meet a basic human need for companionship and support.*

- *Real friends are essential if you want to avoid the negative effects of loneliness and social isolation.*

- *Friends help you to stay healthy and live longer.*

- *They also improve your overall well-being and state of mind.*

- *Having friends helps you to mature and develop as a person.*

- *A true friend allows you to be your true self.*

- *Friends bring purpose, meaning, and enjoyment to life.*

- *Friendship is based on unconditional love and mutual respect.*

- *There are always opportunities to make new friends.*

2

THE SECRET TO FINDING NEW FRIENDS

I f you go looking for a friend, you're going to find they're very
scarce. If you go out to be a friend, you'll find them everywhere.
– Zig Ziglar

**It would be very easy for me to say that the best way to
find new friends is to go out more, but it's a lot more
complicated than that.**

You can be in a room filled with 100 people and still find
yourself unable to strike up a conversation with any of them.
If you remember my zumba class, I had plenty of opportunities to get to know others better, but I didn't.

Hanging out at bars or joining gyms is not always the solu-
tion, although I'm not suggesting that you stay locked up at
home either. What I really mean is that, just because you go
to parties, bars, or take up a hobby, it doesn't guarantee you
will make friends any easier if you don't know how to.

Some people have a knack for getting on with others wherever they go and find it easy to talk to total strangers,
although that isn't a sign they have a lot of good friends. In

reality, you don't have to be super-chatty to make friends and, often, the harder you try, the less success you will have.

My advice is not to hunt for friends whenever you go out because you are setting yourself up for disappointment. Friends will come to you, at the right time, in the right place. It's quite an organic process that you definitely can't force, although you can do certain things to up your chances of connecting with people who you may create friendships with. But first, let's address where you are going wrong.

Why don't you have any friends?

This is a good time to think about why you haven't made any new friends recently. Apart from practical reasons, such as moving to a new city where you don't know anyone, or starting a new job/university, there may be more deep-rooted explanations.

It could be that you are pushing people away, even though you aren't fully aware of it. I realized that I wasn't giving off the right vibes when going to the gym, as if I had put a wall up between myself and the outside world. In effect, I didn't give the appearance of being friendly, so no one felt like approaching me. I couldn't see it at the time because I was too involved in the daily grind and routine.

People take non-verbal cues from the way you behave and aren't going to make the effort to get to know you better if you have a big 'Keep Out' sign stuck on your forehead.

It starts with the way you present yourself. Are you smiling or sullen? Welcoming or intimidating? Arms crossed or open? Engaged or distant?

We learn how to read body language and facial expressions of others way before we learn how to read and write, and we respond appropriately. A baby can distinguish between a smiley face and a sad one from as early as five months old. Think of it this way: would you approach someone who looks tight-faced, stiff, and stern? You are more likely to keep away from them if you know what's good for you.

We don't necessarily act this way intentionally. It can often be a defense mechanism because we want to protect ourselves. It's a kind of passive-aggressive behavior that may stem from deeper feelings of unhappiness that we haven't addressed.

Those emotions could go back to your school days or be a result of present circumstances. It may be that painful memories of not being picked for the school swimming team are still with you, and you haven't been able to resolve that feeling of rejection.

You certainly don't want to stick your neck out and risk getting rejected again. It might be that you have just lost your job, which has stripped you of your self-esteem, making you come across as miserable or even hostile. In essence, you project everything that you feel inside to the world outside.

Depending on what you are going through in life, you may make a lot of presumptions about other people too: that they won't be interested in your problems, won't be able to understand you, or don't share much in common with you. Those assumptions have more to do with how you feel about yourself than any reality.

Low self-esteem, which I talked about a lot in my previous book, **Love Yourself Deeply**', can manifest itself in many ways. It is particularly obvious in a social setting, where you don't feel worthy of love and respect.

You prefer to keep your head down because you tell yourself that you aren't that interesting. This can also make you appear aloof and distant – not the way to attract friends by any means.

These are just some of the more personal reasons why you may find it difficult to make friends, so it is worth spending some time to ask yourself these simple questions:

- How do I feel about my own self-worth?

- What is my body language telling others?

- How often do I smile at other people?

- Is my behavior still affected by a bad experience from my past?

- How friendly do I look?

Once you have thought about the above points, you will have a better idea of how your emotions and mindset are influencing the way you come across to others. It's a great start to understanding what you need to change so that you give off nothing but positive, friendly vibes from now on.

Where can I find new friends?

My answer to this question is, EVERYWHERE! Friendships can be formed under the most unusual circumstances, at the most unexpected moment, with people we may never have thought were 'our type'.

I think that a lot of us are under the wrong impression that in order to make new friends, we have to go to parties, join clubs, take up a sport, or become a member of an interest group. This really isn't the case because it's one thing to meet new people and quite another to know how to form friendships. In actual fact, you don't have to go very far or take up some extreme sport in order to find friends. They may be right in front of you and you just can't see them.

Think about your daily routine and as you do so, consider the opportunities for making new friends. It all depends on your age and circumstances so I have created a sample profile for you to get the idea.

Let me introduce you to Steve.

He's 24 years old, has just moved to Edinburgh from a small town, works for a big car-rental company, and loves football.

- Each morning, Steve takes the same bus to work, alongside the same commuters.

- He has 3 work colleagues, all of whom are married with children.

- He speaks to several clients throughout the day either by phone or in person, some of whom are regular customers.

- He visits the same coffee shop each lunchtime as it is near to the office.

- On weekends, he likes to explore the city on foot and watch TV at home.

Steve is young, active, working, and a nice guy. But he feels very lonely. What would you recommend that he does to find new friends, based on the information above?

As you can see, there are ample chances for him to create a rapport with someone, from the moment he steps out of his house.

- He could strike up a casual conversation with a fellow commuter on his daily bus route.

- He could make an effort to get to know his colleagues more. Even though they all have children, they may have nephews, nieces, or siblings nearer to Steve's age that he could be introduced to.

- Some of his regular clients may now know him by name and if he engages in friendly conversation with them, he is creating a window of possibility to develop friendships outside of work.

- His local coffee shop probably serves the same clients, at the same time as Steve goes there, every weekday. That is another opportunity to strike up a conversation with one of the regulars.

- Steve is out exploring the city at the weekend, which offers him many options for meeting people. Whether he is asking directions, discovering something about local history, or checking out cool stores, being pleasant and chatty may lead to new acquaintances.

- Although he likes to stay at home on Sundays and watch TV, enrolling in a 5 a side football club will definitely give him an opportunity to meet new people with the same interest as him.

Your routine will probably be completely different from Steve's, but I am sure that you will have equal opportunity to make new friends. If you consider how many people you come into contact with on a daily basis, there is always the possibility of getting to know them better.

You see, you don't need to start signing up for expensive annual gym subscriptions or joining a pottery class to find new friends. Start by looking around you and be more open to the idea that you already have a number of chances to meet people.

Even if you are currently working from home, or looking after young children, you still have a routine, right? Whether that is going to your local store, enjoying a walk, taking the kids to daycare, or having Zoom chats with clients and colleagues, there is an opportunity to meet people. All you need to do is find a way to begin a conversation and get to know someone better.

We are going to discuss the art of small talk in Chapter 3, but for now, let's just focus on ways to meet and engage with others. As I mentioned above, there are countless ways for us to make new friends without having to go to any great length or expense. Just by stepping out of the house, you are going to meet people, even if they don't seem particularly interested in you at first. Believe me when I say that we are ALL looking for real, human connection even if we seem disengaged or distant.

Of course, there is a fine line between being friendly and being obtrusive or even creepy, but you can't let that stop you from reaching out to new possibilities. If your intention is genuine, people will recognize that and if they don't respond as you would wish them to, don't take it to heart. Just like you, many people find it difficult to open up and prefer to bury their heads in their iPhones instead.

Going back to Steve, there are many other things he can do to find new friends that go beyond his daily routine. I am going to list some of them below, plus others that you may be able to apply to your own circumstances. I'm sure you can think of many more once you put your mind to it, but here are a few to be going on with:

Your daily commute

I used to take the same metro every morning to go to the office and would see the same faces, sitting in the same seats. Would it have been weird for me to start chatting to one of them? Maybe, but one day I just decided to say 'Good morning' to the woman who had been sitting opposite me for the past ten months and that completely broke the ice.

We ended up chatting all the way into the city center and I discovered that she lived very close to me and we both went to the same hair salon. From that day on, we became good friends and often meet up for coffee on weekends. If I had never said that simple 'good morning', we would still be strangers.

You aren't going to hit it off with everyone so don't expect to. If the other person shows no interest in keeping the conversation going or is unresponsive, don't take it as a personal failure. Simply let it go and change seats the day after – there are plenty of other people to strike up a conversation with.

Who knows – you may find someone with the same interests as you, but you won't know until you try.

Take a walk

Apart from exploring by yourself, there are other ways to meet up with new people. In Steve's case, he could join one of the guided tours of the city, which you will find organized in most places these days. He will definitely meet a new group of people who share his interest and will have plenty of opportunities to chat during the tour.

Some of them may also be newcomers in town who are out to meet people, making it a very easy way to form new friendships. If you enjoy walking in nature, you'll find many activities organized by local hiking groups.

All you need to do is put your name down, turn up on the day, and be open to new possibilities. You may even find that people will approach you out of curiosity, wanting to learn more about you, which is great!

Find out what's going on

As you walk around your town or city, check out flyers for events near you. There is always something happening and if a particular event piques your interest, go for it. You might find out about a music concert, a talk, or an exhibition and, depending on what you are into, it could be a fantastic chance to mingle with others who share your passion.

Many museums and local attractions offer free entrance on certain days of the week or month, so you don't have to pull out large sums of money to attend. You will be amazed at how many people frequent museums, galleries, and similar venues alone because they don't have any company.

Strike up a conversation about the exhibits on display and you may just find a kindred soul who is more than happy to engage in conversation with you.

Pursue your interests

What do you love doing? Are you into playing a sport, keen on collecting rare books, interested in wine-making? Whatever it is that fuels your passion, find out where and when it takes place and go.

You may feel a bit awkward at first but it's quite possible that you will find others who are also alone and have joined the activity for the very same reason as you – to make friends.

Whenever you join a group environment, it's important to remember that you don't have to do anything other than be yourself. There is no need to try to fit in or pretend to be someone you aren't: acting naturally is the only way to form genuine friendships and find someone who appreciates what you have to offer.

As with any activity, having the right mindset from the beginning will determine how successful you are. Turning up with the expectation that no one will be interested in you is not the way to go about things. Take the stress out of making that first step by simply telling yourself, "I'm going to have a good time and just see what happens."

Create your own network

Why wait to be invited by others when you can organize social events yourself? This is where social media really comes into its own because you can form your own groups and invite people to join. For example, if you are keen on eating out, you can organize a 'Dine & Meet' event. Make a page on Facebook and invite people to join. Set a time and date at a local restaurant and encourage your contacts to attend. Make sure you emphasize it is a friendly get-together for anyone interested in trying out a particular eating spot and see how it turns out.

There are plenty of other groups out there that cater to individual interests but maybe nothing that appeals to you, so create your own.

Check out online social platforms

There are some very well-organized online social platforms that focus on bringing people together and you have nothing to lose by trying them out. Most major towns and cities organize events for members, so all you need to do is sign up to receive details of upcoming events. Platforms like Meet-

Up.com use your location to tell you what's going on near you.

I just checked my feed and found out that there are so many interesting events coming up in my town. I saw Acting Courses for Beginners, Content Creators Coffee Time, a 2-Day Meditation Workshop, and a Kayaking Weekend, to name but a few. All of these seem like activities I would enjoy and I am absolutely certain that the majority of attendees won't know each other, or may have only met once or twice in the past.

This is an awesome way to create new social circles and to meet folk who enjoy the same things as you. There are similar groups wherever you are and I know some are global, such as InterNations.org. Let's say you have moved to a new country and want to connect with other expats. The platform organizes a wide range of social events, no matter where you are, and basic membership is free.

Many of the people you meet at these organized gatherings will be in the same boat as you and are keen to establish a network of friends from back home. This kind of opportunity is the ideal scenario in which to form new bonds and all you have to do is show up with a smile and a willingness to mingle.

Meet your community

There may be a lot going on in your community and getting involved is a great way to meet the locals and form authentic relationships with those living close by. You may decide to do some voluntary work – volunteers are always needed in all walks of life – so think about your skills and offer them up. Hospitals, community centers, and local charities are great places to check out and you may find something worthwhile to do in your free time as well as meet like-minded people.

You can also check our organizations such as Volunteer-Match.org and Idealist.org, both of which show you where voluntary (and sometimes paid) work is needed in your location.

Network with your peers

Depending on your profession, you may find events like trade fairs and conferences taking place that you can attend. The advantage to this is that you already have at least one thing in common with other attendees: your job. You definitely have something to talk about, and linking up with fellow professionals is not only good for you careerwise, but may also bring new friendships.

As a remote worker, you may often feel isolated, so look out for coworking spaces, where you will find people in a very similar situation to you who are also keen to interact.

If you aren't currently employed, there are still ways to connect with people in a similar situation to you. You can take advantage of any free events, festivals, or happenings going on in your area and socialize with people of the same age or background.

If you have young children, you may discover parent groups that meet up regularly, which offer both support and a chance to talk about your problems in a welcoming space.

Get a dog

This may sound weird, but if you are able to, having a dog is a fantastic way to meet others. You will have to commit to getting out of the house at least once a day for your four-legged friend's daily exercise, which can also mean meeting other dog owners along the way.

Dog parks are the perfect place for both dogs and humans to get to know each other but even by walking down the street, dogs do attract attention.

I wouldn't suggest this if you really don't have the time or resources to be a responsible owner but if it is possible, consider the advantages and check out your local dog shelter. If your living conditions don't allow you to have a pet, you could always volunteer at one of the shelters themselves, where you are bound to meet a lot of new people and potential friends of both the four and two-legged kind.

Step out into the real world

A lot of the time, people who have no friends find themselves in that position because they don't know how to socialize and this is increasingly true for the younger generation. Instead of getting out there, millennials have grown up behind a screen and learned how to connect very well with others in the virtual world.

It's not that they are anti-social, but more that online connections can be much less complicated and require little effort. Technology can even bring solace to someone who feels lonely, which shouldn't be knocked, but it's not the only way to make friends.

The idea of going out to a bar by yourself can be pretty intimidating, and I wouldn't recommend it if you have little self-confidence or are naturally shy. It's not easy at all to turn up alone at a social venue and the whole experience may make you feel extremely awkward and uncomfortable. As a society, we are still getting used to the idea that people, especially women, who are enjoying a solitary drink aren't there looking for a pick-up so it's a call that you will have to make yourself.

There are plenty of other places to socialize anyway, many of which I have mentioned above.

A lot depends on how capable you are of walking into a situation where you know no one and if you lack that skill, it can actually be learned. We'll delve into that topic later on.

In the next chapter, we are going to look at an issue that holds many people back when it comes to making new friends. That's the problem of how to get people to like you.

Not everyone you meet is going to instantly warm to you but if you have the tools to allow them to get to know you better, you have a greater chance of success.

After all, you are a likeable person, so now you need to let others see that too!

Key Points:

- *By understanding why you have no friends, you can begin to change that.*

- *Your facial expressions and body language play a vital role.*

- *You can find friends everywhere if you know where to look.*

- *Your daily routine, interests, and passions can lead you to new friendships.*

- *Make use of community meet-ups and social groups to get to know more people.*

- *Network with peers, use apps, or organize your own social events.*

- *Get out into the real world whenever you can.*

❧ 3 ❧

THE ART OF SMALL TALK

*T*he best way to become good at small talk is not to talk small at all — Keith Ferrazzi

Now that you have some ideas of how and where to meet new people, the next step on your journey to making friends is to learn how to strike up a conversation with them.

This is the moment that most of us absolutely hate:

What should I say first?

What if I sound stupid?

What if I get a rude response?

What if I get no response?

What do I say after that?

Ummm....

Honestly? Most people hate small talk because it is usually predictable, boring, and can even be annoying. After an initial, 'hello', what else is there to say? Well, most of us like

ıt the weather, which is a safe but bland ice-
rtunately, if your opening line is something like,
oday," then you aren't really opening up a
all.

.c doing is making a statement and giving the other
person little leeway to respond other than by saying, "Yes, it's
lovely," or something to that effect.

Not only are you making any further engagement extremely
unlikely, but you are not showing a genuine interest in that
person. Even if you approach them with a different opening
line, such as, "Looking forward to the weekend?" you are
most likely only going to get a 'yes' or 'no' answer.

That's the conversation falling flat on its face from the offset.
It's also the awkward moment when you feel like climbing
under a rock!

So what IS the secret to small talk? It feels so frustrating,
doesn't it? You want to meet new people and you have the
opportunity to do so, but can't think of anything to say to
them other than, "It looks like it's going to rain," or "Have
you worked here long?"

Although they may be perfectly acceptable things you would
say to a stranger, that doesn't mean that they are going to
help you make friends.

The truth is that small talk is usually made up of boring,
meaningless, forgettable conversations that bring no value to
you or the other participants. I'm not suggesting that it is
completely useless if you know how to use it the right way. It
can lead to a longer conversation where you develop a better
relationship with someone or be the first and last words you
will ever say to them.

Although you are trying to get to know someone better, if you don't go about it the right way, you aren't likely to learn anything about them and maybe never will. How exactly can you learn to master the art of small talk and move forward to having a more meaningful connection with another person?

There are two things that you need to consider here and I want to talk about each one in more detail. Apart from the importance of WHAT you say to someone, HOW you say it is extremely relevant and I would like to address that issue first.

Before we get into the nitty-gritty of how to make your conversation sparkle, let's take a look at how your demeanor, behavior, and the way you speak are crucial to your friend-making mission.

What is your body saying?

Bear in mind the fact that our brains process information at lightning speed and most of the cues it works with are non-verbal. Your tone, body language, rate of speech, emotional mood, and so on, are all analyzed instantaneously, giving the person you are talking to a lot of useful information.

This determines whether or not they want to engage in conversation with you at all. If someone who is clearly intoxi-cated comes over to talk to you, for example, you aren't going to want to give them the time of day. This is an extreme example of how important a person's outward behavior is. Equally, if you invade someone else's personal space, that can be a real put off too, and you need to pay attention to that.

Personal space. There is a comfortable amount of invisible space that we all need to maintain in our interactions with others. Breaching that can have serious consequences. The less you know someone, the more space you will need to give them in order for them to feel safe.

It's not a good idea to overstep the line in your efforts to appear friendly because that will have completely the opposite effect. The more intimate you are with a person, the less personal space you and they will be claiming but we still have some way to go before that.

You know yourself how it feels when someone you don't know gets too close to you and it can be pretty uncomfortable. A good rule of thumb is to think of it in terms of keeping someone at arm's length, which is an expression we use that literally works in this case. Obviously, as you get to know the other person better, that distance will eventually dissipate but if you are still unsure about what behavior is acceptable and non-threatening, here are some things to bear in mind:

- You should never touch anyone you don't know.

- Unless you know the other person well, stand at least 4 feet away from them.

- If someone leans away from you, that probably signifies that you are making them feel uncomfortable, so back off a little.

- Don't lean over someone's shoulder or strain to take a peek at what they are reading – this is extremely rude and annoying.

- Don't sit right next to someone in a theater or seated venue if other chairs are free. It's only really acceptable if there are no other seats available.

Body language. When you approach someone for the first time, your body is doing the talking for you before you even open your mouth. Imagine how you would react to a stranger walking up to you based on first impressions and you will soon realize that there are some basic behaviors that can make all the difference.

Take a look at the pointers below and practice each one in the mirror at home. It may sound silly, but it's a great way to correct giving off negative vibes next time you want to start chatting to someone.

- Check your posture. It should be relaxed, with shoulders down, but not slouched. Let your arms hang casually by your side, rather than crossing them as if you are shielding yourself ready for battle.

- Knowing how to use a firm handshake that doesn't squeeze the life out of someone is important. This is another thing you can practice by yourself, shaking your own hand to feel the difference between a confident gesture and an aggressive grab.

- Always maintain good eye contact, without making it look as if you are glaring. What is the difference? Well, a nice level of eye contact means you will hold the other person's gaze for a few seconds at a time. If it is a continuous stare, you will make them feel very unsettled. Again, practice this technique in the mirror as if you were talking to someone else until you feel you've got it just right.

- Throughout the conversation, try to keep your hands relaxed by placing them on your lap or even in your pockets. This also stops you from fidgeting and fiddling, which may portray nervousness or insincerity.

- It goes without saying that you shouldn't be constantly checking your mobile phone throughout the conversation. There is nothing more annoying and it does not convey to the other person that you are genuinely interested in them. Put your phone to one side or, even better, place it out of sight and focus on the person in front of you instead.

Getting rid of fear. It's difficult to know what to say to a complete stranger to break the ice and just the thought of it can fill you with great anxiety. You are very likely to make a total mess of things as a result, with your nerves getting the best of you and making you sound like a complete buffoon. The way to get around that is to reduce your stress levels before you even approach another person and that's something you can work on at any time of the day.

Firstly, you need to change your mindset about meeting new people. After all, what is the worst thing that can happen when you talk to someone? The fear that you have built up inside your mind is usually unwarranted and even if someone is extremely rude to you, at least you will realize they are not the kind of people you want to have as friends.

Their antisocial reaction shouldn't prevent you from engaging with others after that or keep you from opening up.

Secondly, even if you are a shy, introverted person by nature, it is possible to enter into a pleasant conversation with someone if you go into it stress-free. This not only applies to new people but to those you already know, whether they be colleagues, peers, or acquaintances.

Your anxiety may make it extremely difficult for you to engage with others and you probably use tactics to prevent that, such as looking totally absorbed in your phone.

Anxiety grows from within us and usually has nothing to do with our external environment. It is a collection of bad memories that you believe will repeat themselves in the future. This is not the case and once you accept that, it will take a huge weight off your shoulders.

It can also stem from your lack of confidence and low self-esteem. Again, believing in yourself is the key to entering into any social interaction with positivity and enthusiasm.

What is the worst-case scenario? Imagine what you will, but the most probable outcome is that someone shows little interest in you. That's not the end of the world by any means. After all, you don't immediately like everyone you meet, do you?

Many people, just like you, would actually love to have someone to talk to, especially at social events during which a lot of strangers have been thrown into the same room. You are not the only one who finds it hard to begin a conversation, so stop thinking that you are and just relax!

What are you saying?

Now that we've ticked those boxes on how to behave and get rid of your anxiety, let's get to the heart of the matter and look at ways to crack the small talk code.

When I go walking through my local country trails, the only other people about are fellow walkers, most of whom I don't know. As our paths cross, there is always a nice exchange of 'hello' or 'good morning' to signal that we are passing friends, not enemies.

Pleasantries like that serve a very good purpose and needn't be any more involved than those few simple words. It's the same with small talk: it doesn't have to be a profound statement or a summary of your life story. It's simply a way to break the ice and, depending on the response, you can take it to another level if it seems appropriate.

Here's the thing - the more you fret about talking to someone, the less likely you are to have a positive mindset about it. Just chill out and be yourself, approaching any conversation with a genuine desire to learn more about the other person.

This is your mission - not to bore someone to death about your morning stuck in traffic or the ins and outs of your stamp collection.

The art of small talk actually lies in talking less and listening more.

Ask questions. After the initial, 'Hi. How are you?' you may feel stuck. The trick here is to ask open-ended questions that require more than a 'yes' or 'no' answer. For example, it is easier to engage someone in conversation if you say something like; 'How did you end up working here?' This prompts them to talk about their past and where they worked before, giving you a chance to open up the dialogue.

Think of questions that begin with 'why?', 'how?', and 'what if?' to encourage a full answer that you can then expand on. It's OK to make closed-ended questions too because you don't want the other person to feel you are interrogating them, but the trick is to find the right balance of both.

Be curious. As I said above, showing a genuine interest in the other person instead of talking about yourself is a much better way to get to know someone. By doing so, you are also taking the stress out of wondering what to talk about, because you simply let them do most of the talking.

In addition, while they are telling you about themselves, you are learning more about them and may find that you have one or two things in common that can feed further discussion.

Most people love the opportunity to talk about themselves, so be curious and ask them. You will usually get a very positive response, as long as you don't sound like you are prying or being too intrusive.

Listen carefully. Show that you are following what the other person is saying by maintaining eye contact and giving an occasional response such as, 'I see', or 'Yes, I know what you mean'. The person you are talking to will understand how engaged you are, which encourages them to open up even more.

If you start fidgeting, looking around you, or yawning, that isn't going to make the other person feel that you are really interested in them. It goes without saying that you shouldn't keep checking your phone during the conversation either. Would you be happy to start chatting to someone who is constantly glancing at their mobile screen? Probably not.

Be enthusiastic. Whenever you approach someone that you don't know or want to get to know better, go into it with the right attitude. Show enthusiasm in learning more about them and look at the conversations as an opportunity to connect with them.

If you are willing to make the effort in the first place, embrace it as a positive experience that you can learn something from, rather than seeing it as the equivalent of walking over hot coals.

Share your stories. Be prepared and willing to share information about yourself without dominating the conversation. You don't want to make the other person feel that you are cross-examining them, so you need to interject with your own personal experiences.

Your aim is to offer hooks that the other person can latch onto, thus prolonging the interaction. Tell them about something funny that happened to you, or share interesting facts about yourself that will make them curious and want to get to know you better.

Recognize the cues. You don't have to be a genius to know when someone is getting bored during a conversation. If they start fidgeting or looking disinterested while you are talking, that's a clear sign that they are disengaged.

That being the case, you can either change the subject or bring the conversation to a close with a graceful parting statement like, 'Well, it was nice to meet you', or 'OK. I need to go but it was lovely to meet you'. Be gracious as you bow out and don't let the other person's disinterest take away from the whole experience or make you feel like you failed in any way.

In Chapter 2, I mentioned several opportunities that you have to open up an interesting dialogue with someone in your daily life. Below, I've added some examples of the kind of open-ended questions you can ask to learn more about the other person as well as the prompts that will get you past the small talk phase.

I've used the scenarios from Steve's life although all of the following can be adapted to your situation and I am sure you will be able to think of many more ideas once you have read them.

You will find an initial ice breaker, followed by questions that can lead to a more involved response.

On your commute:

The traffic's bad today, isn't it?

What do you think about the plans for the new metro/bus station?

How did you end up living here?

Where are you originally from?

34

What's your hometown like?

At work:

How's your day going?

What did you think of the meeting/workshop?

What brought you into this profession?

What's your experience been like so far?

How do you think I should go about asking to change departments?

In the coffee shop:

I just love the coffee here, don't you?

Can you recommend any good Italian restaurants in town?

Are you into PC games or do you prefer board games?

How do you like spending your time off work?

Where did you go on vacation this year? How was it?

Out and about:

Have you been on a tour like this before?

Is this your hometown or are you new here too?

How often do you go back home?

Are there any good bookstores you could recommend near here?

What's your favorite book, and what do you like about it?

In general, there are many things you can say to break the ice, depending on where you are. Here are some further examples that you may be able to adapt to your particular situation:

1. What's your story?

2. How is work going?

3. How do you know about this place?

4. What's your boss like?

5. Where did you live before moving here?

6. What is usually the highlight of your day?

7. Have you ever thought about making a career change?

8. What would be your dream job/lifestyle?

9. How are you finding the food?

10. Having fun?

11. What are you doing this weekend?

12. What are your favorite restaurants around here?

13. What local sports teams do you follow?

14. What would you recommend from the menu? Got any favorites?

15. Did you see that viral YouTube video about the funny cat?

16. What TV shows are you into?

17. How often do you play sports?

18. What's your favorite drink?

19. What's your dream car?

20. What streaming service do you use?

Depending on how the conversation goes, there are hundreds of subjects that you can bring up which may fuel further discussion. If you feel comfortable and see that the other person does too, end the conversation by asking if you can exchange phone numbers or connect on social media. This shows that you are interested enough to want to see them again or that you enjoyed their company. If that is the case, say so. A simple comment before you part can be something like:

It was lovely to meet you. I hope to see you again.

Have a great day and let's do this again sometime.

I really enjoyed our chat and would love to get together again with you.

I'd love to meet up with you another time.

It's been great talking to you.

Can I give you my mobile number?

Can I have your number to keep in touch?

What's your profile name on Instagram/Facebook?

If the other person feels comfortable with you, they will probably be happy to share their contact details. If not, don't take it to heart.

They may still be unsure but what's certain is that if you bump into them again, you can take up where you left off and hopefully get to know each other a bit better. Let things flow naturally and simply see how it goes!

Although this is not a book about dating, you can use all of the above strategies to find a romantic partner, if that is what you are after. Whether you are approaching a man or a woman, be mindful of your body language and how you come across to them.

Although physical attraction may be your primary motivation, don't shoot yourself in the foot from the beginning by coming across too strongly. Relax, be yourself, and show genuine interest in getting to know them better with the help of the questions mentioned above.

One thing I want to mention before we leave this chapter is that often you will find other people approaching you with the intention of starting a conversation. This can be equally stressful and cause you to freeze up completely.

The way to get around this is by trying not to answer their questions with one or two words, but to give fuller replies that can lead to a deeper conversation.

So, when asked, 'How are you?', instead of giving a short response of, 'Fine' or 'Good', try to make it longer by saying something such as, 'I'm good thanks. I was just wondering what the weather will be like next week as I have some time off work'.

When asked, 'Where are you from?', don't just say, 'London'. Give more information, such as, 'I really love it there because there is so much to see and do. I used to live near Hyde Park and there was always some event or festival going on in summer.'

If asked, 'What did you do on the weekend?' instead of saying, 'Nothing much', expand a bit to allow the conversation to flow with something like, 'I usually go shopping at the weekend but my car's in the garage so I stayed home and watched Netflix'.

The main thing is to give a genuine response that reflects who you are, what you like to do, and how your life is at this moment.

You never know – you may make a lifelong friendship simply by talking about yourself for a few minutes. Connecting with people is much easier when we open up and allow them to get to know us.

Now that we've looked at how to use small talk and turn it into something bigger, I want to walk you through the steps you can take to make it easier for people to get to know you better. The secret lies in opening up even further throughout the conversation and helping them to like you.

If someone is interested enough in you, you will find this a lot easier than you think.

The more you spend time with people, the more they will get to know you. If your initial contact is for just 5 minutes, they may learn a mere 5% about you. When you next meet, it might be for a few hours. That gives them the opportunity to learn even more about you.

As you hang out together more frequently and for greater lengths of time, they will get to know you 100%, just as you will get to know them.

That's the beginning of a promising friendship!

Key Points:

- *Small talk doesn't have to be painful.*

- *Your body language speaks volumes.*

- *Be aware of personal space, facial expressions, and behavior.*

- *Change your mindset to remove anxiety.*

- *Ask open-ended questions to avoid one-word answers.*

- *Enthusiasm, curiosity, and listening go a long way.*

- *Always offer to exchange contact details if you feel the chat went well.*

❧ 4 ❧

THE SECRET TO ATTRACTING PEOPLE WHO WILL WANT TO KNOW AND LIKE YOU

friend is one who knows you and loves you just the same. – Elbert Hubbard

There is only one way for people to get to know you better, and that is to know yourself first.

If you can be honest and accept who you are, embracing both your strengths and weaknesses, this makes it a lot easier for others to learn about you too.

Once you have gotten past the small talk and established some kind of connection with the other person, opening up about who you are is the next step to making friends.

You don't need to be perfect (no one is) but by having self-awareness, you can admit your weaknesses, recognize your strengths, and enable others to appreciate you and like you. This is the crux of all good relationships but it applies more than anything else to friendships.

As we already mentioned, people choose who they want to be friends with. It is one of the few social bonds in life that is based on pure choice – if I like you and get on with you, and the feeling is reciprocated, we will most probably become friends.

That's why it's super important to make sure you feel comfortable in your own shoes first. When people get to know you, they will either warm to you or not, and that's OK. It may be that when you meet someone new, they discover they have nothing in common with you, don't like your views, or aren't impressed by your personality.

When you stay true to yourself and aren't trying to please others, you are more likely to make authentic, genuine friendships based on mutual respect and esteem.

Who am I?

This isn't one of those profound existential questions that needs some deep philosophical thought. It's simply a question that I would like you to think about before you take a pen and paper to make an outline of yourself. Apart from your age, gender, and so on, it's about knowing your likes, qualities, dreams, and passions. It should be easy for you to do as you know yourself better than anyone else, right?

Below, you'll find an example that will help you to make your own personal profile. In this case, I'm going to introduce you to Jill, a good friend of mine who I met by chance when she backed into my car in a parking lot. (Like I say, you never know when or how future friends will appear.)

NAME: Jill

AGE: 35

OCCUPATION: Nurse

STATUS: Single

HOBBIES: Tennis, horse riding

CHARACTER: Kind, caring, affectionate, trustworthy, shy, stubborn, worries too much

LIKES: Going to the cinema, making sushi, dogs, crosswords

DREAMS: Opening an animal rescue shelter, visiting Japan

It may be that although you find most of this exercise relatively easy, you have difficulty identifying your character traits. That's because we find it hard to be honest with ourselves and pinpoint our weaknesses, as well as our strengths. Give it a shot anyway and once you are done, you can always add to it if you think of anything else.

Once you have a more definitive picture of who you are, this can be the springboard for helping others to get to know you better. It is good to talk about yourself, as long as you don't monopolize the whole conversation. For example, your occupation can be of great interest to others.

Whatever walk of life you are involved in, it can be used as a conversation starter and the more you talk about it, the more you are allowing the other person to get to know you. If you aren't employed, you can talk about your ambitions and if you are studying, sharing your reasons for choosing a particular subject can be very insightful. Meeting people who have the same interests or hobbies as yourself can be a great way to connect.

You both have something to talk about and can instantly relate to one another. If you have little in common, that isn't necessarily a bad thing, although it does make it harder to establish a common dialogue at first.

I got to know Jill back then because, although she had accidentally bumped my car, she told me she had been in a hurry as she was late for her tennis lesson. I used to play the sport myself and wondered where her lesson was and how much it cost.

We got chatting and before I knew it, we had arranged to meet up the following week for a friendly game. I also appreciated the fact that Jill hadn't just driven off after smashing my tail light and had waited around to give me her insurance details. I liked her integrity and honesty.

It wasn't long before we became very good friends, even though I know nothing about horse riding or making sushi!

Knowing me, knowing you

In the last chapter, I mentioned how useful it is to ask open-ended questions in order to get to know the other person better. If you want them to get to know you too, you have to be prepared to open up. That may sound scary to many of you, because you don't like the idea of feeling exposed or vulnerable.

Your past experiences in life might have left you feeling let down, used, or even betrayed. That can be hurtful but here's the thing: the longer you hold on to the pain, the longer it will stay with you. If you really want to make new friends, you must be prepared to reveal something of your inner self, although you don't have to spill the beans from the first contact. You can do it gradually once you have established a greater level of trust.

At this stage in the game, all you need to do is talk a little more about the easy stuff, such as what you like to do in your spare time, any hobbies, and interests.

Finding common ground. So, the person you are talking to mentions that they have just moved to town? Great! Ask them where they are originally from and how they are adjusting. Tell them that you have just gone through the same experience and you will be able to compare notes. Perhaps they tell you they love dogs. Excellent – you have been thinking of adopting one and can talk about the dog you had as a kid... anything dog-related will do.

Be passionate. When you talk about things you are genuinely interested in, you will find yourself opening up more. If the other person asks about your job, tell them about why you love it so much and if you hate it, talk instead about your dream job or your ambitions – your passion will give them a better idea of who you really are.

You don't need to go into all of the in-depth details but by talking about something that inspires you, you are allowing them to form an emotional connection.

Be honest. You don't need to reveal your deepest, darkest secrets at the outset, but that doesn't mean you shouldn't be honest. When you weave a tangled web, it will eventually come out into the open, so it's much better to be genuine from day one. If you do feel the impulse to lie or 'embellish' the truth, think about why that is. Do you not feel good enough?

Are you trying to prove something to someone? Honesty is always the best policy and you can simply avoid touching on subjects that make you feel uncomfortable, rather than lying about them. At the end of the day, if the other person doesn't like the real you, how can you expect them to be your friend?

Getting people to like you

We all want to be liked, but friends need to like us even when they get to know our bad points. You may have had friends in the past who were unreliable, couldn't keep a secret or were useless with money, yet you liked them regardless.

Being liked isn't about portraying yourself as some kind of perfect being. We all have imperfections and are still worthy of friendship. My take on this is not to try too hard to be liked by everyone. You have a much better chance of forming genuine friendships if you concentrate on showing an interest in the other person rather than trying to impress them. Be liked for who you are, despite all of your flaws.

There's a very famous book by Dale Carnegie that was first published way back in 1936. The title of it was 'How to Win Friends and Influence People'. It became a huge best seller because it tapped into the reader's desire to be liked.

His book's message still rings true today, with one of its most famous quotes being: *"You can make more friends in two months by becoming interested in other people than you can in two years by trying to get other people interested in you."* That begins with how you handle the conversation and the way that you engage with others, so here are the main pointers:

How to create an engaging conversation

Once the ball is rolling, there are several things you can do to keep up the momentum. As long as you are interested in the other person and get the impression they are interested in you too, the following strategies will help you to establish a natural flow in your conversation.

Use the person's name

This may sound obvious, but when you keep mentioning someone's name, it makes you appear even more focused on them, which is exactly what they want. It's a tool that sales-people use a lot as they try to connect with potential buyers and is definitely an effective way to establish some kind of rapport.

Use verbal confirmation

This is also known as 'active listening', where you repeat what the other person is saying to show that you are paying full attention. For example:

Jill: I saw this amazing movie at the weekend. It really touched me, especially at the end when the couple got back together.

Me: It made you emotional, really?

Jill: Yes, it was so good, and Nicole Kidman played the part brilliantly.

Me: Oh, you like Nicole Kidman? I love her too.

Jill: Yeah, she is really great.

As you can see, it's not difficult to maintain this kind of dialogue. All you are doing is showing the other person that you are paying attention to what they are saying. When you echo them, you are validating their opinion and feelings, as well as finding the opportunity to share your own.

Listen

I mentioned in Chapter 3 that it is much better to listen more and to talk less. Even if you are chatty by nature, take some time to let the other person speak and be responsive to what they say. By allowing them space in a dialogue, you are showing them interest, curiosity, and respect. What's not to like about that?

Know it all

When responding to another person, don't act as if you know everything about everything (even if you do). There's nothing worse than a know-it-all because not only do they make us feel inferior, but they are also just downright annoying.

Stay humble and be prepared to say, "I don't know," every now and again, which can help to put the other person at ease. Instead of trying to impress, practice 'being' impressed by what you hear and stay curious to learn more.

Be funny

You may not be a natural comedian but injecting a little humor into the conversation will certainly win people over. Everyone likes to have a laugh and if you can manage to raise a smile, your company will be genuinely appreciated. Laughing at yourself first and foremost is a great way to endear the listener to you, so tell a funny story or make light of a problem and see how it changes the mood.

Admit your imperfections

It's OK to tell someone that you aren't good at this or that, or are unable to achieve something you desire. Human connection springs from being vulnerable, so don't underestimate its power. At the same time, pointing out the flaws of the person you are talking to is not the way to go. Less judgment and more understanding are both crucial at this stage of your budding friendship.

Mirroring body language

By subtly mimicking another person's body language while talking to them, you are encouraging them to like you more. If you copy their gestures, expressions, and posture, you are making them feel that you are following what they say and have empathy with them. The result is that they will find you more likable and relatable, no matter what you are talking about.

Personal hygiene

I don't want to have to be the one to tell you this, but if you have bad breath or neglect your personal hygiene, that can be a real put-off. Do take care of yourself by showering regularly, keeping your hair and/or facial hair well-groomed, and make sure your overall appearance is clean and tidy.

Chew on a mint to overcome bad breath if you have to, and feel free to use antiperspirant or deodorant as and when. If you look good on the outside, you will feel good on the inside, which will add to your confidence and make you even more approachable.

Getting closer to someone isn't just about the conversations you share but also requires doing things together. Shared experiences are definitely going to help you bond more so it's a good idea to initiate future plans. Whenever you meet up with someone as your friendship progresses, make suggestions about engaging in activities that you can both enjoy together, depending on your interests. It can be as simple as grabbing a coffee next week to going to see a basketball game together at the weekend.

My Friend Jill invited me to a tennis tournament, which is something we both enjoyed. In turn, I asked her if she wanted to go to the theater with me, and she happily agreed. Whatever activity you decide to do together, you will give the other person a chance to get to know you more without having to try too hard.

Opening up

It's only by opening up to people that you can strengthen bonds and maintain a relationship. This takes time and doesn't come easy to all of us. When you do feel that the other person will listen to you without judgment, perhaps you can begin to share some more intimate thoughts with them.

You will be surprised to see that by doing so, you will gain a different perspective. You may even receive advice or counsel that can help you to overcome any personal issues you have been dealing with. By sharing your experiences, you will feel less alone and this is a true gift of friendship.

If you still find this difficult to do, it may be a serious stumbling block to you making friends. There are some things you can consider to help you to overcome your fears in the company of the right person, enabling you to be more open and less inhibited.

1. Identify what you are afraid of.

Are you holding back for a specific reason? Did something happen to you in the past that has left you feeling overly self-protective? Were you subjected to rejection or shame? Any one of these is enough to make you reticent about revealing yourself so take it one small step at a time and don't force yourself to negate your feelings.

Once you pinpoint what past experiences are causing you pain, you can allow yourself to let them go as they serve no purpose now.

2. Learn to express how you feel.

When you have thought about where your lack of trust is coming from, try to express that by saying, "I feel anxious because..., I find it hard to open up due to...." You will be surprised to hear how many other people not only understand you on hearing that, but will also tell you that they feel the same way.

Remove the idea in your mind that no one will understand you, or will think you are being silly. Being true to yourself and expressing how you feel can actually help you to gain wonderful friends in the long run.

3. Be personal, not vulnerable.

You can talk about many personal aspects of your life without the fear of feeling vulnerable. It could be about your favorite music, what you like to do in your free time, what motivates you in life, what you like about your neighborhood – all personal subjects that don't leave you feeling emotionally exposed. If you aren't up to it, avoid talking about anything in your life that creates a sense of vulnerability. This may include topics related to your health, medical conditions, family dramas, relationship worries, fears, or hardships.

4. Take your time.

Don't rush into overpowering the other person with your life story. Give the relationship time to grow and develop but be mindful that if you only engage in small talk, you aren't allowing him or her to get to know you better.

In general, a first meeting should be kept light while on your second get-together, you can begin to broach more personal subjects. In subsequent meetings, it's OK to talk about what's on your mind, what challenges you are facing, or how you feel.

You can go from a casual conversation to a deeper dialogue after establishing that this person is someone you feel able to share things with. Once you do so, you will develop a much closer bond. After that, the onus is on you to maintain that friendship, which is something we are going to look at in the next chapter.

No matter what age you are or your personal circumstances, it's never too late (or too early, for that matter) to form a life-long friendship, beginning today.

The more someone gets to know you, the easier it will be for them to like you so don't hold back. Trust your instinct and be open to new possibilities!

Key Points:

- *Knowing yourself is the secret to allowing others to know you better.*

- *Willingness to learn more about the other person is crucial.*

- *Be honest, passionate, and find common ground.*

- *Engaging conversation will encourage others to like you.*

- *When you are able to open up, you can create greater intimacy and trust.*

HOW TO FORM LIFELONG FRIENDSHIPS

T*he only way to have a friend is to be one.* — *Ralph Waldo Emerson*

One of my best friends lives in Australia, so I only get to see her every two years when she comes to visit the UK. We speak now and again on the phone or message each other, but live very different lives, in very different time zones.

This makes regular communication a bit difficult but as soon as we do meet up, it feels as if we have never been apart. We talk about everything, and I feel a strong sense of familiarity, warmth, and trust when I am with her.

That's the magic of friendship and I know that even though she lives thousands of miles away, I can call her a true friend.

This relationship is a good example of how we can have lifelong friendships even with people we hardly see. There is a bond there that neither time nor distance can break: one which was formed many years ago. Friendship really is like a good wine that takes time to mature but if it is strong enough, it won't let you down.

The truth is that we all need meaningful relationships in our lives and friends are perhaps the only people who we can truly be ourselves with. Unlike family members, colleagues, or other acquaintances, friends are people who you can rely on through thick and thin.

No matter what happens, they will be there for you because they want to be, and not out of any sense of obligation or duty. That's the nature of friendship, and if you have managed to make friends like this, you should hold onto them.

Forging such friendships takes time, effort, and a genuine desire to live up to your side of the bargain. After all, you can't expect others to be your best buddies if you aren't also committed to the relationship 100%. It's a two-way connection based on mutual trust, understanding, and loyalty that we need to work on to create those long-lasting bonds. This chapter is dedicated to exactly that, and I'd like to begin by looking into how you can nurture a deeper relationship with new friends who may turn out to be lifelong allies.

Firstly, it's a good time to consider what being a good friend means to you. How many of the things below do you think are essential qualities someone needs to exhibit in order to call them a friend?

- Honesty

- Love

- Giving

- Compromise

- Forgiveness

- Faith

- Support

- Dedication

- Respect

- Thoughtfulness

- Loyalty

- Anything else?

The above list is quite demanding, isn't it? We expect our friends to portray most, if not all of the above, but we have to be prepared to offer the same if we want the friendship to last the passage of time. If you are in the process of making new friends, which of these qualities are you able or willing to bring to the relationship? Can you be a good friend?

It takes two to tango, and you can't expect the other person to offer you the hand of friendship if you aren't prepared to reciprocate. Fairweather friends will come and go in your life: they are OK to hang around with when everything is rosy, but when the going gets tough, they disappear.

The point here is to create bonds with people who won't bail on you when you need them, which is what true friendship really means.

Your negative past experiences may have left you feeling distrustful or disappointed, making you cynical about forging new relationships. That is perfectly understandable but you have to get over those negative preconceptions if you want to move forward. We all need friends in life, as I mentioned in

Chapter 1, and you can't make new ones if you are stuck in the past.

Some of your difficulties may lie in the present, believing that everyone else already has a close circle of friends. This can make you hesitant about reaching out to someone, without realizing that many people simply hang out with others so they don't feel lonely.

It could be that you have gotten so used to being alone that you don't believe you need anyone or can't break the habit. It's OK to live alone, but having friends can bring so much more into your life if you are prepared to open up to new possibilities

A lot depends on where you find yourself at this moment in time, as well as how old you are. In Chapter 8, we are going to take a look at ways to make friends if you are a teenager or young adult, but a lot of what is covered in this chapter can also apply to you.

Many of us will have found ourselves in a strange town, school, neighborhood, or even a social situation at some point in our lives where we knew absolutely no one. Instead of seeing that as a negative, we can use it as an opportunity to get to know people, and once we have begun to forge those new friendships, we can work on making them even stronger.

How do we do that?

There are some basic requirements of friendship, if it is to stand the test of time. When you think about your old friends, no doubt you will have memories of sharing both the good and bad times. They may have been the only ones to support you, encourage you, and be there to support you when no one else would.

Hopefully, you did the same for them, creating a strong bond that you still cherish, even if you have lost touch with them now or aren't able to meet up with them. Hopefully, you will know what it feels like to have that one person in your life who you can trust without hesitation, someone who you got along with so well that you miss them even today.

You can create strong friendships like this, and you will find 15 pointers below on how to do so:

Befriend yourself first. You know that this is paramount, don't you? As I've said many times before, if you don't like yourself, it's going to be tough to get others to like you. Self-acceptance is the key here, forgiving yourself for your past mistakes, and acknowledging who you are.

Choose your friends wisely. One of my favorite quotes is, "Just because you are thirsty, it doesn't mean that you should drink poison." Being alone is no fun but making bad choices about who you strike up friendships with can be catastrophic.

You can choose who to befriend, so make it based on your needs, wants, and likes. Stick around those who give you joy, love, and fulfilment rather than people who bring toxicity into your life. This applies to virtual friends too, who can have just as much impact on how you feel.

Be yourself. You may not be liked by everyone, and that's OK. The people who do like you are the ones to keep in your life. A true friend will allow you to be yourself and accept you as you are, without wanting to change you. By the same token, don't expect others around you to change or be something they aren't. This isn't the foundation for a friendship based on mutual respect and honesty.

Practice empathy. You may not be able to solve any of your friend's problems, but you can show that you understand how they feel. Sometimes, that's all we need in order to feel better, so put yourself in their shoes and let them know you feel for them, even if you can't fix what's wrong.

Be kind. Kindness is a very underrated virtue in a world defined by big gestures, money, and status. But it's the simple acts of kindness that touch others the most because those actions come from the heart and are totally altruistic. You will know how it feels to experience the kindness of others, so be the one to share a kind gesture with a friend and enjoy doing so. You will never regret it.

Give your time. There is nothing more valuable in life than time. I recently read that a true friend is the one who spends time with you even when they would rather be somewhere else. In some ways, that rings true, because friendship requires a certain amount of sacrifice, which may often be your time. By making time for your friends, you are showing how much you really care about them, and that is priceless.

Don't take them for granted. You wouldn't expect a friend to ask you to abandon your own needs in order to fulfill theirs so don't do it to them. No one likes to be taken for granted and this leads to a feeling of being used. Show your appreciation for anything a friend brings into your life but respect their boundaries while doing so.

Say thank you. Part of showing gratitude means saying thank you: two words that can say so much. They let the other person know how much you appreciate them and you can do it in a number of ways. Leave them a nice message, buy them a small gift, or treat them to dinner. Whatever it is, it will reinforce the bond that you have and show them what a positive difference they make to your life.

Say sorry. We don't always do the right thing, but we can always apologize for that. Being honest about your mistakes and having the courage to say a simple 'sorry' is the mark of a true friend. If your friend needs to apologize to you, accept it with grace and let them know you forgive them, instead of making them feel even worse. Accept and move on.

Nurture trust. This is the number 1 reason why many friendships break down, never to be patched up again. If you can't trust your best friend, who can you trust? When someone confides in you, it is an unspoken rule that you never betray them or break their confidence to anyone. This also applies to more practical issues like turning up on time, collecting those cinema tickets, or doing anything that you have promised to do.

Ride the storm. True friends won't abandon you when you need them the most, and you need to be there for them too when they need it. No matter what situation they are in, how bad they are feeling, or what problems they face, being there is the other side of the friendship coin. It's not only enjoying the good times together but also weathering the storm when things get rough.

Respect your differences. Your friend doesn't have to agree with you on everything or hold the same views. If you can be open-minded, you are recognizing their individuality and allowing them to be who they are without judgment. This is the liberating essence of friendship and something you no doubt will appreciate yourself. Letting those differences exist without feeling the need to be right all the time is the best way to avoid conflict and arguments.

Be a good listener. Lending an ear to a friend is one of the most important gifts you can bring to the table. You don't always need to give advice, find solutions, or provide feed-back. Simply by hearing them out, you are offering them a space to express their worries or concerns, as well as their hopes and dreams. Listen with intent and let them know you hear them, without having to say a word.

Celebrate their successes. When your friend achieves something significant in their life, celebrate with them and show genuine happiness for their accomplishments. There is no room for rivalry or jealousy in friendships so enjoy their moment of glory as if it were your own. They will appreciate that more than you know.

Accept their choices. Sometimes, we need to make choices in life that have the potential to ruin a long-standing friendship. Even if they have to move to Australia, that doesn't mean that you need to stop being friends. Encourage them to pursue their dreams and wish them well, without taking their decision as a kind of personal rejection. If they are a true friend, their happiness is important to you, and vice versa.

Setting boundaries

One thing I do want to touch on in relation to bonding with others is to remember that you need to maintain boundaries. Although you want to be there for them and will run at the drop of a hat if they need you to, it's also crucial that you set boundaries. Just as in any healthy relationship, the dynamic will not work if you allow codependence to form. What does this mean?

It's very easy to let a friendship develop into a codependent relationship in which all borders have disappeared and there are no personal limits. These limits are crucial because they help us to remain independent and able to see to our own needs and feelings.

When they don't exist, we become too dependent on our friends and lose the ability to think and feel for ourselves. You cannot expect any one individual to meet all of your needs and if you do so, this can lead to a loss of identity for both or either of you.

This dependency on another person can be harmful to your overall well-being, like a drug that you become addicted to. Usually, the friendship will shift from one of mutual respect to that of 'giver' and 'taker' and you could find yourself on either side.

Maybe your friend always needs rescuing, or you spend most of your time trying to fix their problems, while your own are ignored. You might begin to feel exhausted after hanging out with them or are unable to find peace of mind as you are too busy meeting their emotional needs. They could rely on you too much, leaving you feeling suffocated and dreading the time you have to spend with them.

All of these examples can signal the end of a friendship, so it's vital to be aware of the dynamic and change the relationship if you feel the need to. You can do this in several ways:

Think about how you got here.

When did you or your friend start to manifest these codependent tendencies? Was it triggered by something specific or were warning signs there from the beginning?

Practice the act of putting yourself first.

See to your own needs and wants first. If you don't feel like going bowling tonight, it's OK to say "no." This gives a clear message to your friend that you are prioritizing your needs and also shows them that it's acceptable to do so.

Find the balance.

Explain to your friend how you feel and see if you can work together to reset the balance. If that isn't possible, then the friendship may not be sustainable.

Be your own person.

Although it's wonderful to have friends in our lives, we don't need to be connected 24/7. If you feel that you are over-relying on your friend to fill your life, try to find some other interests that don't include them and let them know your motivation for doing so.

Good friends will stick with each other through thick and thin, but won't be totally dependent on the other. Seek to create friendships with healthy boundaries in which both of you are aware of each others' needs.

That authentic, trusting connection will mature over time, based on mutual respect and a genuine desire to see the other person is happy and fulfilled. Be there when needed and ask the same in return, safe in the knowledge that you have an unshakeable bond that truly enriches your life.

Good friends come in all shapes and sizes and if the bond is strong enough, it will last forever. They bring a unique quality to our lives, helping to shape the people we are today and often determining the people we will become. When I think about the friends I have now, I am very conscious of the fact that I don't dedicate enough of my time and energy to them.

This is probably something we all have in common, as our busy lives get in the way of spending quality moments with those we love to be around.

In the next chapter, I am going to introduce you to something called the Pareto Principle in order to overcome that. It's all about how much effort we make and what results we expect to get for our endeavors, so stay with me as we delve into how to make the most of our treasured friendships.

Key Points:

- *Being a good friend demands specific qualities and actions.*

- *Friendships are built when we understand what being a friend means.*

- *Follow the 15 pointers to create strong friendships.*

- *Setting boundaries avoids codependent relationships.*

- *There are ways to establish and maintain healthy friendships.*

❦ 6 ❧

MAKING FRIENDS WITH THE
80/20 RULE

*I*t is not shortage of time that should worry us, but the tendency for the majority of time to be spent in low-quality ways - *Richard Koch*

I met Jake a few months ago. He was one of those start-up tech geeks who had come to my office to talk me through digital advertising.

He was a really outgoing, chatty guy, who was obviously very passionate about his job and we got talking about where he was from, his background, and so on.

Jake told me that, although he had a lot of friends, work prevented him from hanging out with them as much as he would have liked. He also confessed that some of them didn't even get in touch with him anymore because he was always turning down their offers to meet up.

It turns out that Jake was spending most of his time building his business and neglecting his friends, leaving him feeling frustrated and desperate to turn things around, although he didn't know how.

You may have the exact same problem yourself, putting all of your energy into your career, or even your family, leaving no time to invest in your relationships. After a while, you might notice that they stop calling you, don't message you as often, or aren't available when you finally have time to meet up with them.

I know how this feels because I've also been guilty in the past of getting caught up in the daily work routine and weekend burn-out syndrome. The thing is, people aren't accessories that we can put on or discard when we feel like it.

We need to give time to any relationship if we want to sustain it, and this applies just as much to friendships as it does to our relationship with a spouse, partner, children, or other family members. So, how exactly do we make the most of our time and commit to nurturing friendships when our work/life balance is heavily out of sync?

One way to approach this, I have found works for me is by using something called the Pareto Principle. It's an idea named after the Italian economist Vilfredo Pareto, who noticed back in 1895 that about 80% of Italy's land belonged to 20% of the country's population.

Since then, the principle has been used mainly in the business world, focusing on the fact that 80% of results or consequences come from 20% of effort or causes. The Pareto Principle is also known as the 80/20 rule, the law of the vital few, or the principle of factor sparsity.

Simply put, all it really means is that 20% of your efforts will probably lead to 80% of your success in many spheres of life. In the context of this book, we are going to look at how using the principle can allow us to nurture and sustain close friendships to the best of our abilities.

Obviously, your friends are important to you and whether you are trying to make new ones, or hold on to those already established, the 80/20 rule will give you the tools to do so, no matter what your circumstances are.

When it comes to forming new friendships, think about this: if 80% of your efforts are getting you nowhere but 20% of what you do gets positive results, do more, much more of the 20%.

If you are always trying to impress, talk too much, or are overbearing, and you're not getting the results you want, notice how unsuccessful this kind of behavior is and cease doing it.

It's easy to measure - how many friends have you actually made by talking about yourself all the time? On the other hand, how many new friends have you made by offering a good ear, talking less, and showing empathy? I think your answer to that will tell you exactly why the 80/20 rule is so useful.

Looking at your relationships using the 80/20 model

Let's say that you have connected with a few new people and would like to deepen your friendship with them. You want to get to know them better and also want them to get to know you. What's the best way to do this using the 80/20 rule? Begin by asking yourself the following questions. You don't need a calculator or have to start counting fractions. Just give a rough estimate based on an 80-20 ratio by following your gut feeling.

1. Of all the people you know, who are the five to ten people you spend the most time with?

2. Does spending time with these people make you a better or a worse person?

3. Pick the one or two people you enjoy being with the most. These are the 20% who make up 80% of your social engagement and are probably the most interesting and fun people to be with.

4. Spend more time with the 20% who make your life better, and less time with the 80% who don't.

Once you have a clearer idea in your mind about who you enjoy being around and those who makes you less happy, then you can begin to work on resetting the balance. Take the time to do an 80/20 analysis on your current and potential friends to make sure that you're building relationships with the right people, otherwise, it really is a waste of your time.

How can you build on those relationships?

Our time is so limited, isn't it? When we do have the opportunity to enjoy ourselves, we want to make sure it's with the right people. That requires us to make conscious decisions that will help us to use our time wisely.

Although the 80/20 principle isn't only about time management, it can be useful to apply it in this way once we have established our needs and goals.

Jake, for example, had very little free time. By his own admission, he had become somewhat of a workaholic, clocking up 12 hours a day or more on his projects. I asked him how productive he was working so many hours. He thought about it for a while and finally admitted that he didn't really feel that motivated or inspired when it got to 7 or 8 in the evening.

Basically, he was less productive as the day went on. If he had only applied the Pareto Principle to his working life, he could have worked fewer hours but have been more focused on what he was doing, resulting in a better performance.

It's the same with friendships - if you focus on one hour of quality time together rather than 5 hours of chatting to them on social media, you are much more likely to develop a closer bond. You can begin to work on having a better interaction by following my 3-step plan, which is outlined below.

The 3-Step Plan

1. Set your goals

Often, we go about life in a sort of random way, not really having any direction or goals. We seem to leave a lot to chance and then complain afterward when things don't go our way. Sitting by yourself in a coffee shop instead of going over to chat with the guy or girl also sitting alone is a wasted opportunity. In addition, waiting around for your friend to call is not the way to go about developing any kind of relationship. You have to plan, making sure that you use each chance you have to form new friendships and maintain them.

Set yourself goals, instead of leaving things to fate. Make them specific and doable, rather than vague and impossible. Jake said, "I'd love to see my friends more, but I'm too busy." He needed to change that statement to: "I want to see my friends more and will set a time and date for that to happen." This entails working more productively, spending less time working half-heartedly, and giving priority to his personal needs.

See how easy it is?

Following the Pareto Principle, Jake needs to focus on the 20% of his daily habits that bring him 80% efficiency and happiness. He also needs to get rid of the 80% of his routine that only brings around 20% of the value to his life.

2. Plan your goals

You may bump into a friend in the street or see them in your local store by chance, but more often than not, you will need to be proactive if you want to be sure of getting together. Making plans is the best way to do this, which will entail prioritizing what is important to you.

If you wish to arrange an evening out, you have to plan ahead for that. Leaving things to the last minute may be your usual style, but where has that gotten you so far?

When it comes to planning anything, concentrate on putting the things that you enjoy doing at the top of your list. Sure, you have responsibilities that aren't always fun which you have to include, so take these as given and draw up a plan that maximizes your free time.

When you have narrowed it down to who brings you 80% of your happiness when you are around them, draw up a plan that could look something like this:

- Call or message the other person once a week if you are just forming a new friendship

- Call or message once a day if your relationship is growing

- Reduce the amount of screen time you share in favor of actual face-to-face meetings

- Suggest to meet up once a week

- If they don't live locally, make a suggestion to get together once a month

- Set a time and date for the meet-up and suggest a location

- Confirm the meeting in advance

- Turn up on time

3. Evaluate other priorities

Bearing your goals in mind, it's time to look at everything else in your life that could conflict with that. Are you being pulled by other people that you don't enjoy being with into spending time and energy on them? What do you do on a daily basis that brings you 80% unhappiness?

What do you do that brings you 80% joy? You need to find the 20% that improves your daily routine and focus on those.

Make a list of your priorities and consider which ones you could maximize or reduce. If you like, you can number them in terms of impact, with 1 being the least impactful and 10 being the highest. Your list could look something like this:

- Commuting 2 hours to work and back

- Visiting parents/relatives daily

- Working overtime to impress your boss

- Cooking and cleaning

- Scrolling through social media

- Watching TV or streaming

- Exercising

- Chatting on social media

- Grocery shopping

- Procrastinating (putting things off that you would rather not do)

You can add to this list, depending on your lifestyle and habits. When you have considered everything, ask yourself which of the above you can handle differently in order to release more of your time and energy. I would say, for instance, that I used to hate grocery shopping. I found it very tiring and couldn't stand waiting in long queues when I'd rather be somewhere else. I thought it was a necessity until I realized that I could order everything I needed online and have them delivered to my door. That was truly liberating, and such a small change to make, allowing me to meet up with my good friend Sue for a chat over a pizza. Magic!

A word about procrastination

There is nothing more time-wasting than procrastination. It's the equivalent of walking into quicksand and slowly sinking. Putting off what you could do now until later because you don't enjoy doing it is in total contrast to the Pareto Principle. The 80/20 rule doesn't say that you should ignore doing what you need to but is about finding ways for you to deal with each task effectively so that it doesn't drag on and on, robbing you of both time and happiness.

There are many ways to beat procrastination, but for the purpose of this chapter, let me just say that 2 hours of concentration will give you a much better outcome than 8 hours of idling about and avoiding the task at hand. If you need to do something and can't avoid it, put it at the top of your task list and see to it before you do anything else.

Establish effective habits

Avoid those things in life that don't bring you happiness using the 80/20 principle and break bad habits such as binging, using harmful substances, drinking too much, spending hours on social media, over-sleeping, not exercising often enough, and so on. If you don't enjoy what you are doing or are experiencing anxiety and stress, now is the time to deal with that because the after-effects can be long-lasting.

You can think about:

- What habits are causing 80% of your problems?

- What things are causing the most stress in your life?

- What experiences bring you 80% of your happiness?

- What small daily habits can increase your level of happiness (e.g., getting out more, meeting friends, etc.)?

Once you have narrowed it down, continue to use the Pareto Principle to help you stay true to your goals and plans. It's not that difficult to change habits and routines when you understand the benefits of doing so, and the 80/20 rule is a very clear benchmark for that.

If we apply the rule to relationships, it appears that 80% of our happiness comes from just 20% of the people in our lives. This implies that there are a lot of people around us who add very little or nothing to our sense of joy.

These could be old friends, new friends, or people we just hang out with. Once you pinpoint who these joy-killers are, try to gradually remove them from your life, without conflict or stress.

I had an old friend, let's call her Nadia, who I met when my kids were at kindergarten along with hers. We kind of became friends as we seemed to have some things in common (i.e., kids at the same school), and I found her fun to be around. She had a wicked sense of humor and was always upbeat. We would meet now and again, and the more we did so, the more I noticed that she could also be quite condescending. She would often make snide comments about what I was wearing, or remark on my 'lack of style', and I began to enjoy our meetings less and less.

The truth was that, apart from making me feel bad about myself, she wasn't adding anything to my life anymore, so I decided to gradually remove myself from that 'friendship'. I stopped calling her and when she would call me, I simply explained I was too busy to meet up. Eventually, we lost touch and I can honestly say that the friends I made after her bring me so much more contentment. No one needs a 'Nadia' in their life.

There will always be people who you can't strike up a relationship with, and that's fine. There's no such thing as a perfect fit with everyone, so focus on those you truly value and respect rather than hanging out with people just because you think you have no other option. Make choices based on YOUR likes and needs, not those of others, and you will be much more likely to find friends on your wavelength.

Once you have established the kind of friendship that fulfills you, it's a good idea to make sure that you maintain a healthy balance based on mutual respect. It could be that, after a while, you sense things are not going the way you would like them to. You may begin to feel taken for granted or are always the one who has to make the effort to call the other person and arrange meeting up. We are going to look at how to deal with such developments in the next chapter.

Until then, remember: 80% of your results come from 20% of your actions!

Key Points:

- *The Pareto Principle can be applied to making new friends and keeping them.*

- *80% of results in life come from 20% of our efforts.*

- *Follow the 3-step plan to achieve your friendship goals.*

- *Establish healthy habits using the 80/20 principle.*

- *Remove the people in your life who bring you more sadness than joy.*

7

HOW TO GET YOUR FRIENDS TO CONTACT YOU MORE

A *one-sided friendship brings exhaustion and there's no one deserves to be sucked dry – Euginia Herlihy*

There's a lot of truth in the saying that 'friendship is a two-way street' and we've probably all been in relationships that often feel more like one-way roads to nowhere.

I know from personal experience that when you have to do all of the leg work, it can get tiring and demoralizing. If you find that it's always you who has to call up your friends, organize the get-togethers, or make changes to your schedule to accommodate theirs, you probably start to feel that this is unfair after a while.

You wouldn't be wrong there — true friendships aren't built on one making all of the effort while the other sits around doing little to contribute. Sooner or later, you are going to wonder if you are really friends at all.

And to make matters worse, if you get replies like, "I'm busy, I'll call you later," when you contact them, and they never do, that sucks. The same goes for messaging: there's nothing more infuriating than texting a friend, only to be ghosted by them.

Although this kind of one-way effort can indeed be a sign that the friendship isn't as solid as you think, there may be other factors playing out that you aren't aware of. Some people don't feel comfortable taking the initiative, for example, and others are used to having someone else do all of the running around.

You need to get to the bottom of why you are the only one trying to sustain and nurture this friendship, which we are going to look at below. After that, I'm going to give you some useful tips to help redress the balance and to know when it's time to call it a day and move on.

I'm not going to tell you to simply end the friendship or get involved in an all-out row about why they never call you. This type of approach causes nothing but hurt, conflict, and even shame or guilt on both sides. Instead, I want you to think about how valuable that person is to you and how committed you are to making the friendship work.

No one likes to be taken for granted but often or not, our own sense of insecurity or lack of self-esteem can cloud our judgment. Also, any past experiences of being in a hurtful relationship can make us super-sensitive and too quick to judge others, without giving them a chance to explain themselves.

A lot has to do with the way we 'think' people should respond to us, and how we should behave in return. Add to that, the fact that we are all familiar with taking on a certain role in our relationships and don't realize that we need to step up or change our approach.

One-Sided Friendships

One-sided friendships are exhausting and some of the tell-tale signs are things like:

- You always have to take the initiative to meet up. If you don't, nothing gets arranged.

- They only contact you when they need something.

- You always need to go to their place but they'll never come to yours.

- You always need to fit in with their plans.

- You are always there for them but they aren't there for you when you need support or help.

- They never ask how you are.

- You show your friend kindness and generosity but get nothing back in return.

- They only ever talk about themselves.

Remember my 'friend' Nadia from Chapter 6? She was going through a rough patch with her husband at one point and needed some time away so she asked me to join her on a weekend break.

I was excited at the prospect of spending a few days of relaxation although I knew that she would probably also want to talk through some of her problems during that break.

What I didn't expect was for her to monopolize the conversation for the whole two days, going on and on about her problems without even asking me how I was doing. I came home feeling emotionally drained and used. It seemed like she only cared about herself and selfishly assumed that I was prepared to listen to all of her problems without any consideration for me.

Being a good listener is fine, but when the conversation is totally one-sided, it can call into question how much your friendship really means to this person and can make you feel like a door-mat. That's how I felt, and I'm sure you will have experienced something similar. Maybe when you do call your friend, they spend all of your phone time talking about themselves, when you could actually do with a listening ear yourself. They may never be available when you make suggestions to meet up, but demand that you drop everything to get together with them when they feel like it.

Showing kindness to your friend is also great, as long as they appreciate it and would act the same way with you. If not, that's very unfair. Of course, we don't carry out acts of kindness to get anything in return, but you know the difference between someone being genuinely grateful and someone who is simply taking you for granted.

This can be very damaging to your self-esteem and make you feel as if you aren't deserving of the same kindness and consideration. If you feel like you are bending over backward to please them, it may be a good time to consider why you do that, and what you get out of it.

Listening to your friend's problems is a sign that you care about them, so when you find that they have no interest in your own life, what does that say about them? Perhaps it's part of your nature to be a good listener, but you also need to be able to talk about yourself and to express how you feel, to confide in someone, and share your thoughts with.

Having to take the initiative all the time may be fine with you, especially if the other person is genuinely very busy and doesn't have time to call you first. But, honestly? How long does it take to make a quick phone call or send a short text?

Maybe you need to consider if this other person really is too busy, or if that is an excuse. Whatever the reason for their unwillingness to get in touch, you have to weigh up if it is valid or if it shows apathy on their part towards contributing to your friendship.

If you used to pick them up from work as they didn't have a car, then they ghost you as soon as they buy one of their own, the chances are they were using you. You are right to feel hurt or angry and it's easy to become distrustful of others after that, which may be affecting how you treat any new friends.

Why are you the only one trying to sustain and nurture this friendship?

There are many points we need to consider when experiencing this feeling of 'always having to be the one to make the first move' and wishing that your friends would call you for a change.

As frustrating as it feels, it can also be downright annoying and even make you feel insecure. Does your friend really like you? Did you do something to upset them? Are they trying to give you the hint that they want to be left alone? Do they even want to be friends with you?

Let's think about some of the things that could be going on behind the scenes:

1. Your friend is the kind of person who waits for other people to invite them out first. Not everyone likes to make the first move, and some are more than happy to go with the flow. It's just their style and they aren't aware of how annoying it can seem to others.

Maybe they have never gotten used to initiating anything and haven't picked up on the fact that a good friend will be more proactive when it comes to organizing get-togethers.

2. Your friend may be shy and feel insecure about asking you to meet up with them. Their lack of confidence can be totally misinterpreted by you or others and even though they would love to meet up with you, their insecurities prevent them from calling you.

It can stem from a lot of problems they have dealt with in the past and has nothing to do with you as a person. For some people, it takes a lot of courage to be the one to do the inviting and they may even be relieved when others approach them first.

3. Your friend may not be as focused as you are on arranging a bowling night or grabbing concert tickets. You are always one step ahead of them as you like to organize everything well in advance while they have other priorities that occupy them.

Your friend may have a great idea for the weekend, which they were going to mention to you on Friday, but you've already gone ahead and booked a table at your favorite Mexican restaurant.

4. Your friend may be quite the introvert, who doesn't necessarily enjoy social gatherings and prefers one-on-ones. Someone who is used to being alone can also go a lot longer than a person who is a social butterfly, so their failure to contact you doesn't necessarily mean that they don't want to hang out with you. They simply enjoy their own company and don't feel the need to reach out to you.

5. You may have earned a reputation as being the 'organizer' and your friend has taken on the passive role of waiting for you to make all of the plans. If this is the case, they won't realize that you feel frustrated with them for not calling you

and will assume that it's your job to do the organizing because that's who you are.

6. Your friend may have different responsibilities or priorities in life, which means that they don't always have the same schedule, free time, or peace of mind to contact you.

The demands of their job may leave them feeling drained, or their family situation could put pressure on them that leaves little time for socializing. Not everyone can manage their lives as well as you, but this doesn't infer that they don't want you as a friend.

7. Your friend may not enjoy holding conversations over the phone, preferring face-to-face contact. If you are work colleagues or see each other frequently in class, they may not feel the need to be in constant contact, even if you prefer that.

Not everyone is into texting and many people find chatting over the phone a waste of time. I know people who don't even have a mobile phone, even in this day and age, and others who don't like using social media, which has nothing to do with their desire to have friends.

8. Your friend might feel that they are disturbing you by calling: an impression you may have given them yourself. Not everyone feels comfortable making phone calls without a good reason.

They could be unsure of your relationship, believe they don't have anything interesting to say, or get anxious about where they stand with you. It's possible you are very busy and have ignored their calls in the past or told them you can't talk, which may explain why they refrain from calling you now.

9. Your friend may have different interests to you, so isn't likely to call you to talk about stuff that they think will bore

you. They might know that basketball isn't your thing, so would rather call other buddies who share the same passion as them. On the other hand, they will call you to talk about a new TV program that they know you would like.

10. Your friend's circumstances may have changed. Perhaps they were single when you met and now have a new love interest, meaning that they spend most of their time pursuing that relationship. They could have started a new job or college and need to invest their energy in getting used to that, so they don't get around to contacting you as often as you would like.

There could be many other explanations for your friend's reluctance to call you or organize meet-ups. They could even be trying to deal with problems that you aren't aware of, so try not to jump to hasty assumptions without understanding exactly what is going on with them.

Often, we are projecting a certain type of personality or behavior that gives the wrong impression. For example, calling a friend every day may make you seem pushy or clingy. It could be that you have loads of free time and enjoy chatting on the phone for hours on end, while your friend has responsibilities to meet and can't afford to do that.

A lot of what you are experiencing could be an over-exaggeration you have created in your mind, and this reflects on how you view yourself more than how your friend sees you. Demanding that they call you could be to fulfill some kind of need you have to be at the center of attention and you may not handle feelings of rejection well.

Your idea of what a 'true friend' is could also be re-examined because we often have high expectations of others that are impossible to satisfy. If you believe that being a 'true friend' means having daily contact by phone, messaging, or getting together, then it's quite likely that anyone you befriend will fail your 'friend test'.

We all have lives to lead and although it's natural to want to hang out with friends, not all of us feel the need to do that 24/7. Good friendships are built on mutual respect, which means allowing the other person their space and listening to their needs. If you think it's all about you, what kind of vibes are you putting out to others?

Once you have thought about how you are coming across and what your expectations are, then you can go about redressing the imbalance that seems to be emerging in your relationship. The most important elements are honesty, openness, and communication — reaching out to the other person and explaining how you feel. Let's look below at some other strategies you can apply:

How can you redress the balance?

When you feel that it is only you making the effort in a friendship, there are several actions you can take to put things right. Some of them will test the friendship and reveal how strong it really is. Others are meant to nurture a deeper understanding and hopefully realign your bond with each other.

Talk it through

Communication is the only way to clear the air and move forward. You can't expect to maintain any kind of relationship if you aren't prepared to talk about how you feel, so it's very important that whenever you want to clarify things, you arrange to meet up to talk about it.

Make it clear that you want to meet up with your friend to talk to them and suggest a time and place. Approach the meeting with a genuine desire to reach some kind of understanding, and don't go there in full battle gear ready to attack.

Being over-emotional is also a natural reaction but it is best if you can manage to keep things under control and maintain an amiable tone, rather than shouting or crying. You can prepare what you wish to say in advance if it helps, with statements like, "I've noticed that you don't get in touch with me...

I'd prefer it if you called me more often..." It's not a blaming game here, but a move on your part to explain how you feel and if the person sitting opposite you is really invested, they will listen to you.

Don't forget that they may be going through something that they don't feel comfortable talking about, which could explain their behavior. By opening a dialogue, you let them know how their behavior affects you and also give them the chance to share anything on their mind.

They may feel embarrassed or surprised, but as long as they show a willingness to work things out, your efforts will have been worth it.

Make suggestions

If you are fed up with feeling like it's always you who has to make the call or text, you can approach the subject with some suggestions. Explain exactly what it is that bothers you and propose how that can be resolved. For instance, your friend never texts you or only replies to your messages in one or two words.

Once you point that out, you may find that they simply don't like that particular means of communication. You can then suggest having chats over the phone instead if they prefer.

Perhaps they are always more than willing to come to your place but never invite you to theirs. You can ask if it is OK to visit them and even suggest a specific time and day. You never know — they may feel awkward about having visitors as their home is too small/old/messy, or whatever. If that's the case, respect their boundaries and suggest a meet-up in a coffee shop, park, or any public place.

The point is to make it clear to your friend that you enjoy being in their company and would appreciate knowing that those feelings are reciprocated. There's no use in pressurizing them to behave in a way just to suit you, but you can make suggestions for keeping in touch. Offer them some options such as taking it in turns to call each other, or alternating who arranges what each weekend. That's a great way to bring balance to the relationship.

If your friend is aware of your needs, hopefully, they will make more of an effort in the future to contact you first. If they aren't consistent, it may be that they were simply trying to please you and you will need to consider what your next steps are.

Making plans

If, for whatever reason, you feel that it's always you taking the initiative to make plans, simply stop doing that and wait to see what happens. Instead of arranging nights out, put the onus on your friend to suggest something. If they get in touch, great.

If they don't, you need to ask yourself why that is. Could it be that they are genuinely too busy, or have they become used to you doing all of the leg work? A chat with them can easily clear this up and you will know from their reaction if they are keen to meet up with you or aren't that committed.

You don't need to sulk or start ghosting them. Just be open and explain that you would appreciate it if they could suggest activities too sometimes. Depending on how they respond, you may learn a lot about what is going on with them and even give them the space to take the initiative.

If nothing changes after discussing it, you need to ask yourself how much this behavior is affecting you and what you are willing to accept. You aren't being unreasonable by expecting your friend to organize meet-ups and if they don't seem that bothered, why should you?

Understanding the dynamics

You may have the wrong expectations about your friendship with a particular person. Although you think that you are their best friend (or potential best friend), they may already have a large social circle and you are on the outer limits of that at the moment.

It isn't that they don't like you or don't want to spend time with you but they might overlook you in favor of more established friends. Until you forge a deeper connection, you can't expect to be included in everything so give your friendship time to grow and see how it goes.

It's possible that your new friend feels you won't get on with their social circle, for whatever reason. They may enjoy spending time with you because they can show another side of themselves that they don't feel comfortable revealing with their present friends.

At the end of the day, you don't have to feel like you are competing for anyone's attention or taking anyone's place. Be yourself and don't undermine your value if you wish to earn respect from the other person.

Forming a social circle

Placing all of your money on one horse may turn out to be a lucky move, but can also leave you penniless. Relying on one sole person to satisfy all of your needs is a lot to ask for, especially if that person already has a network of acquaintances.

In reality, no single individual can give you everything you need in life and although it's great to have a few close friends, being too dependent on anyone in particular isn't such a good idea. They may enjoy going to see a movie with you but prefer to go shopping with someone else. That's OK, and you are free to do the same if you wish.

Create a diverse range of friends so that you feel more rounded, instead of waiting for one person to contact you. By widening your network, you have more options and can enjoy being with different friends for different reasons.

There is no need to be left sitting at home, wondering why X or Y didn't call you. Relying on one individual can make or break your weekend, which may leave you feeling bitter and sorry for yourself. By expanding your circle, there will be more opportunities for you to get to know a range of different people and remove your dependence on any one individual.

Adjusting to new friendships

Just because your old college chums used to text you every day, it doesn't mean that a new group of friends will do the same thing. When you begin any friendship, it's important to have an open mind.

Sure, you want to hang out with someone you can rely on, trust, and have fun with, but they may not behave the way your old pals used to. Once you grasp that it's not their thing to text frequently, you can focus on enjoying time together rather than letting any insecurities rise to the surface.

Consider what you are willing to accept in a relationship and how you would like to be treated. You can't force someone else to behave in the way that you would like, but you can determine what is important to you and what you will put up with. If the friendship fades because of that, it isn't something to get angry or upset over. Not everything works out as we had planned and as long as you maintain a healthy sense of self-esteem, you will have lost nothing.

Take a breather

If you feel drained by the relationship, take time out to reassess the situation and to give yourself the chance to evaluate things. By not calling your friend for a week or two, you may even get a clearer picture of how strong your friendship is.

If they call you after a few days asking how you are, saying that they were worried about you, or wondered what had happened to you, that could be an indication that they just find it hard to reach out to you under normal circumstances.

On the other hand, if you don't hear anything from them after a few weeks, you may want to ask yourself what kind of friendship you actually have.

It could be that your friend is not as committed to the relationship as you, and that will become apparent once you take a step back. Some people don't like to feel tied down to one specific person but may still be willing to hook up with you every now and again. If that is acceptable to you, fair enough, but work on developing more meaningful bonds with others who can offer you more than just a casual friendship.

Having friends makes life so much richer but you need to choose them wisely. Not everyone you meet will be friend material and it's up to you to decide what you are looking for in the other person. Choosing those who value and respect you as an individual is paramount. You are worthy of happiness and deserve to have good friends who will appreciate and understand you.

Like most things in life, actions speak louder than words and your relationships need to be reciprocal — if you are doing all the giving, that's not a balanced relationship. If you feel that your efforts are not being met with the same level of enthusiasm, it's never too late to walk away from the relationship. After all, why should you settle for anything but the best?

Letting go of people who don't bring us joy in life is a healthy process and you will be doing yourself a great favor by removing those who make you feel undervalued. You don't necessarily have to make any great declarations or end things with a big argument, although you may wish to express how you feel.

You might prefer to keep in touch through occasional texts or emails, but focus more of your energy on finding real friends who will bring more meaning into your life.

It's not always easy to do that, especially if your circle is limited. If you attend school, college, or university, you may see the same people day in, day out, and find it difficult to strike up a friendship with anyone around you. There are ways to get around that, and I'll be talking you through them in the next chapter.

For now, stay true to who you are. There are plenty of strangers out there looking for a friend just like you!

Key Points:

- *One-sided friendships follow specific patterns of behavior.*

- *There may be many underlying reasons why your friend doesn't contact you.*

- *Communication is crucial to nurturing a healthy relationship.*

- *Making suggestions for ways to address the imbalance can be helpful.*

- *Understanding the dynamic of your relationship and extending your social circle are positive steps.*

- *Give space to the other person and reassess your expectations.*

- *It's OK to let go of friendships that don't work out.*

ꙮ 8 ꙮ

TEENAGERS - HOW TO MAKE
MORE FRIENDS AT SCHOOL,
COLLEGE OR UNIVERSITY

A friend is someone who gives you total freedom to be yourself– Jim Morrison

They say that our school days are the best years of our lives. That may be true for many of us, but for those who struggled to make friends at school, college, or university, those years might have been a total nightmare.

There is nothing worse than being a teenager and having zero friends. The feelings of isolation, not fitting in, or of being excluded, can be devastating and have a knock-on effect for the rest of our lives.

As a parent, knowing that your child is having problems making friends can cause a lot of anxiety and a feeling of being powerless to help.

The fact is that younger people do seem to be having a harder time making friends today than they did twenty years ago, and there are a lot of possible explanations for that. Depending on what age group we are talking about, various factors determine how we build relationships and not everyone has the same coping skills.

The figures are pretty dismal when we examine how young people feel about their friendship status, with an increasingly negative impact on their mental health becoming more and more obvious.

Just to introduce you to some figures, a study by the UK Office of National Statistics carried out in 2018 found that 1 in 10 children aged 10 to 15 often felt lonely. Those in the bottom age range of 10-12 showed a greater sense of loneliness (14%) than older kids in the 13-15 year age group (8.6%).

Similar studies carried out in the US in 2017 also pointed to 39% of high school seniors saying they felt lonely, with 38% of 12th graders admitting they often felt left out and lonely. When it comes to university students, it's sad to see that a recent report carried out during the COVID-19 pandemic found that 20% of year 2 & 3 students in UK universities felt that they had no 'real friends'. For many young people, their time at school or university is clearly NOT the best years of their lives.

As we all know, having friends is crucial to our well-being and helps us to develop and grow. From an early age, friendships help children to learn important social skills such as communicating, coping with problems, self-regulation of emotions, and learning empathy.

In an academic environment, friendships help to form attitudes to learning and affect overall performance. It can make all the difference between success or failure, not just at school or college, but in later life too. It goes without saying that children or teenagers who have difficulty making friends are more likely to underachieve and even drop out of the education system altogether.

To make matters worse, their feelings of loneliness may be compounded by bullying or rejection, all of which are extremely damaging for their emotional and mental welfare.

The good news is that there are plenty of things we can all do to increase the chances of making new friends and get out of the loneliness trap. If you are a young person in a new school or college, you are going to find some sound strategies in this chapter to help you create great friendships.

If you are a parent, you will discover practical tips to help your child overcome their inability to make friends and reduce your stress levels.

I want to take a quick look first at how friendships develop, depending on age, so you have some idea of what is normal. All too often, the stigma of having no friends can be crushing, especially in a world where being 'social' and popular seems to be a big thing.

There's a lot of pressure on young people to be socially active these days, although it's worth noting here that having one or two close friends is much healthier than having hundreds of virtual ones.

How friendships develop

Young children up to the age of 7 usually strike up friendships because of shared circumstances. Joe is in the same class as Mike, sits next to him, lives nearby, and goes to the same karate class.

Their parents are also friends, so Joe and Mike get to see a lot of each other outside of school. They may or may not have a natural affinity for each other and will also be happy to play with another child if the opportunity arises.

From the ages of 7 to 11, more stable friendships are formed based on loyalty, generosity, and fairness. Now Joe places a lot of emphasis on fitting in and feels the peer pressure to be like the others.

He may be part of a small group that requires some kind of code of behavior, with strict rules about who can or can not join. Joe is still friends with Mike but he may also have three to five other kids he calls friends.

From 11 years onwards, friendships have more to do with an adolescent's social, emotional, psychological, and physical development. There's more awareness of the other person's feelings and an increase in intimacy and trust. Now Joe seeks out friends with whom he feels a real connection and he wants to feel loved and accepted. This is the age at which friends can come and go, depending on how strong the relationship is.

Not all children and teenagers are like Joe. Some will have more difficulty in making friends because of certain 'disadvantages'. Although it's not always the case, kids with learning difficulties or communication and/or attention difficulties may find it harder to form friendships. This applies whether you are 7 or 17 and the ability to retain friends can even become more difficult the older you get.

If a child is seen as different by the other kids, it is often hard for them to be accepted by the wider group. Children who are disruptive, aggressive, or exhibit anti-social behavior are also avoided by many others and although they may make friends, often it's with other kids who behave in the same way.

Being bossy or mean can also affect the number of friends they have, and this also applies in adulthood. Kids who are overweight are often the subject of bullying, as well as being unable to take part in some of the normal school activities.

This can lead to anxiety and depression, which, in turn, leads to fewer friends.

Basically, any kid who is different may find it hard to establish strong friendships, including those who are defined by their sexual identity, religion, social status, or ethnic origin.

If any of these issues relate to you, they are very likely to follow you from the schoolyard to the university campus. Unless you get the support that you need, it can be very tough to make friends, wherever you are. Below, you will find some useful advice that can guide you through the friend-making process and help you to find people who love you as you are.

If you are a parent, you need to be there from day one, providing all the help that you can to ensure your child is given every opportunity to develop healthy relationships. Instead of worrying and feeling powerless, it's time to step up your game with the following strategies:

Making friends at school

Kids

Not everyone is brimming with confidence and it's difficult to make friends if you are shy or introverted. You may be with the same kids each day but can't seem to strike up a friendship with any of them.

You can overcome this by looking for those who have the same interests as you and you might just discover that someone you didn't know very well is actually very easy to get along with in an out-of-school setting.

If you love drawing, for instance, join the after-school art group, where you will be able to come out of your comfort zone in a safe environment.

If you love reading, join the book club where you can talk about what books you like with other members.

Ask your teachers if there are any clubs that you don't know about and try them out to see how you go.

Instead of hanging out with people who put others down or who are mean, spend time with those who show kindness and fairness.

You may be tempted to try to make friends with the most popular boy or girl in class, but if they don't show you any respect, just stay away from them.

If you don't think you are particularly good at sport, there are lots of other fun activities you can try out that may lead to making new friends such as joining the table tennis club or even the chess team

Although the thought of going to any social events like school dances may sound terrifying, it is a great way to mix with your schoolmates in a relaxed setting.

Find out if any of your classmates are going to the x or y event, and ask if you can tag along. Invite someone to go with you and even if they can't make it, they will appreciate you asking.

Talk to other people when you get the chance, beginning with a quick 'hello'. You can compliment them on their new school bag or tell them how much you enjoyed the football game they took part in yesterday. Striking up a conversation doesn't have to be intense – keep it casual and take it from there.

Don't hide behind your mobile phone or walk around with headphones. This signals that you are unapproachable, even though you would really love someone to talk to.

Parents

Your child's age will determine how much you can do to help them make new friends at school. The older they are, the more difficult it is to intervene and you definitely don't want to embarrass them or make them feel even worse. Tact and respect are extremely important if you want your child to appreciate your efforts so be mindful of how you go about things.

You can encourage them to take part in team sports, hobbies, games and other group activities. Be there to offer them transport to and from the activity.

Organize regular sleepovers at your home and allow your child to sleep over at friend's houses too.

Invite other kids to your house more often and always make them feel welcome. Arrange for a day out together at a local theme park or to see a movie at the cinema.

Talk openly to your children about social situations and encourage them to share their thoughts with you. Avoid being oppressive when giving advice or stating your opinion, otherwise, the conversation will come to an abrupt end.

Encourage any hobbies that will involve social interaction by providing them with any equipment they need, such as a bike, skateboard, or surfboard.

Let them know that conflict is common in any relationship and give them the tools to resolve their differences with others in an empowering way.

Encourage them to bring their friends over and allow them their privacy when they do so.

Don't be overly critical of their choice of friends or try to manage their relationships for them. Remain neutral when commenting on this one or the other and take care not to convey negative opinions.

Be encouraging, uplifting, and inspiring!

Making friends at a new school

Teens

That feeling of being the new kid on the block can be over-whelming. No one knows you and you don't know them, which can make you feel anxious and extremely awkward. All eyes are on you as you walk into class and as the 'new' kid, you are going to have to earn your place amongst the group.

The first thing to remember is that you have more in common with your classmates than you think, so give them some time to get to know you and you will soon be making plenty of buddies.

Smile when you first meet your new classmates and make eye contact with them to show that you are friendly and approachable, not weird at all!

Take the initiative to start a conversation, beginning with "Hi" and tell them your first name before asking theirs. Often, that's all it takes to get the ball rolling.

You can extend the conversation by paying them a compliment such as, "I love your T shirt. It's so cool." This is a great ice-breaker that will set you off on the right foot.

When you have the chance, you can ask open-ended questions that require more than a 'yes' or 'no' answer. Ask what series they are currently watching on Netflix, then continue with follow-up questions.

Show interest in what your schoolmates do in their spare time and ask them about any social activities going on after school.

Humor is a great way to get people to warm to you so crack a spontaneous joke if you can or tell a funny story about yourself. This is sure to get them laughing and enjoying your company.

Take note of what your classmates seem to be into – what music are they listening to? What books are they reading? Which teams do they follow? Show interest in their pet likes when chatting to them, which they will appreciate.

Be yourself. It's no good trying to pretend to be someone you are not because everyone will see through that pretty quickly. Fitting in doesn't mean having to change – it means finding friends who like you for who you are. If someone doesn't accept you, then they won't make a good friend anyway.

Resist the temptation to be overly accommodating in order to endear yourself to others. Your new friendships should be based on mutual respect and honesty, not superficial behavior or pretense.

Parents

We often recall our own painful memories of being a new kid at school and worry that our children will have the same difficulty in adjusting. Often, there's a temptation to make a fuss about it and to show too much concern. Kids, especially teenagers, often find this intrusive and don't always feel comfortable telling us everything.

If you are genuinely concerned that your child hasn't made any friends at their new school, the following tips will be useful. It's also important to remember that making friends is a skill we begin to learn in our early years and you shouldn't wait until they are teenagers to begin.

Always keep the lines of communication open and let your teen know you are available whenever they need to talk. They may be full of anxiety and could do with a sounding board –

someone who will listen to them without trying to 'fix' everything.

Hear them out and refrain from being a 'know-it-all'. Instead, ask them to reflect on how they feel, how they see themselves, and what is important to them.

In conversation, do some gentle steering that will allow them to understand their emotions. Ask them about their likes and dislikes and give them the space to focus on finding friends who will be a good fit.

Remind them that good friendships grow in time and not everyone they meet will be an instant friend. Latching on to the first person who shows any interest because they feel insecure doesn't mean that they will become bosom buddies.

Practice having light conversations with your child to show them the art of small talk. Maintain an upbeat tone when chatting to them and lead by example, listening with intent when they speak.

Explain that arguments and differences of opinion are natural in any relationship and help them to work on their negotiation and consolidation skills. You also need to practice what you preach and show them that you are willing to be wrong sometimes.

Avoid preaching to them about what you did or didn't do when you were younger. Times have changed since then, Instead, show empathy for their situation and remove any judgment.

If you don't like their choice of friends, be careful about how you share your opinions. Ask why they like hanging out with x or y and initiate a conversation about what having good friends means. Instead of making them defensive, prompt them to look at their friends from a different perspective.

Encourage your teen to have a wide circle of friends and enable them to enjoy a varied social life. Be prepared to support them when they need you, such as driving them from A to B to meet up with their pals and show readiness to give them any other kind of practical help.

Making friends at college/university

Students

Anyone's first year at university can be a daunting experience and often involves moving away from home to a strange town or city. It's one of those watershed moments in life on the road to independence and self-discovery, with the issue of making new friends being a major hurdle to jump over.

The student lifestyle sounds exciting at first, but it can easily become a lonely routine of classes, dorms, and studying if you don't make the effort to meet new people. In order to avoid that, here are some strategies to help deal with university life:

Make sure to attend Freshers week, where you will get a taste of what's going on in the university. Use this as an opportunity to find out about any clubs or societies that may interest you, where you'll find like-minded students. Join the hockey team if you are into that, or sign up to help with the university newspaper.

Try something new – you may discover a new hobby or talent!

If you are staying on campus or in university accommodation, frequent the common areas to get to know your roommates. Remember that everybody is in the same boat as you and are all looking to make new friends.

If you have a communal dining area, you can eat there, which will bring you in contact with fellow students. This type of setting is ideal for making relaxing conversation and getting to know others better.

Get to your classes early and strike up a conversation with people sitting near to you. Ask them where they are from, what made them decide to study this particular course, and tell them about yourself too. You have made a great step towards creating potential new friends.

Ask your classmates what plans they have for after the lesson and suggest going for a coffee or a snack. Most people will be more than happy to have some company as they are feeling just as lonely as you are.

Find out what events are going on in the evenings and at the weekends and if you can't find someone to go with, take a deep breath and go alone. There will be a lot of people you can get chatting to once you are there, some of whom you may recognize from your dorm or classes.

When it comes to studying, make a habit of going to the university library, where you are more likely to meet new people. You can ask what they are majoring in and why they chose this university. Keep the conversation casual as you don't want to come across as intrusive or creepy.

Get involved in a study group and if you can't find one suitable, start your own. Invite people to join and organize to meet up once or twice a week, where you will have more chances to get to know them better.

If you are not into noisy parties or concerts, you could always invite some of your classmates over to watch a movie or for a few drinks. Not everyone may accept your offer, but don't take that as a rejection. They may have already made other plans but would love to come over the next time you ask.

If you are staying in shared accommodation, leave your room door open now and again. This signals to your dorm mates that you aren't antisocial and gives them the opportunity to pop their heads in to say hello.

Get out of your room as much as possible, even if it's just to go for a run or a walk. The longer you stay alone, the more isolated you will begin to feel, which can seriously affect your emotional well-being.

Be prepared to step out of your comfort zone by attending activities you have never tried before, such as campus aerobic classes or baseball. You will find plenty of options and can try anything that sounds like it might be fun and will meet others with the same interests.

If you intend to work part-time during your university year, try to find something that involves socializing, such as in a coffee shop or restaurant either on or off-campus. You will even get to know your coworkers better and may develop a good friendship with one of them.

Be open to meeting people from different backgrounds to your own. University is a great place to expand your horizons and learn about different cultures and identities. Instead of judging people who don't appear to have anything in common with you, learn more about them and let your common interests and experiences help you to bond.

Parents

When the time comes for your son or daughter to fly the nest and spread their wings at university, the experience can be more stressful for you than for them. Naturally, you will have concerns about their welfare and how they will cope in their new life, although feel limited in what you can do to help.

It's up to them now to adjust to their new environment and if they have moved away to another town or city, they also have to deal with managing alone.

Unfortunately, you will not be in a position to monitor how they are doing as much as you would like to and they may not tell you everything that is going on. Despite this, you can probe gently when you have a chance to talk to them.

You can find out if they are having trouble making new friends by casually asking what they have been doing in their spare time. If they reply that they are usually studying in their dorm, dig a bit deeper – perhaps they are isolating themselves too much.

Encourage them to join clubs or teams and explore new interests, letting them know how excited you are for them. If, by the end of the first semester, they don't appear to have developed any extracurricular activities, make sure to open up a conversation about it when they come home.

If they don't mention the names of any new friends, avoid making it a big issue. Instead, act as a safe place for them to air their fears and concerns. Acknowledge how difficult it is to make new friends and suggest ways that will help them to overcome their shyness or awkwardness. (You can use any of the above points).

Avoid face-to-face dialogues if you can – many people feel uncomfortable in this situation and will close up about what is troubling them. Try chatting while in the car together or watching TV – this takes the pressure off and avoids feelings of being put under the microscope.

Don't ask questions like, "Why don't you have any new friends?" or "How come no one ever calls you?" This will only make your son or daughter feel worse if that is the case and cause even greater anxiety. Make open-ended questions instead, such as, "How are things going at uni? Met anyone interesting that you hang out with?"

Remember that not everyone is the same. While you may like having a large circle of friends, your child may prefer to have one good friend instead. True friendship takes time and doesn't happen overnight. Trust them to make their own friends, in their own time, and try to worry less.

A final note

If you are a parent reading this book, it's important to consider that young adults interact differently from when you were their age. With internet access and social media, they have found a way to communicate with each other that we don't always understand or appreciate. I often hear parents expressing concern about how much time their kids spend chatting on their smartphones or laptops but I actually think this is a good thing. Before this ease of communication was widely accessible, kids had much less contact with their friends, so chatting isn't necessarily a bad thing.

It may raise a red flag when it seems to be the ONLY communication they use, but as long as they are attending school or college, they will be interacting face-to-face with others. You can be pretty sure of that.

It's also useful to remember that teens are at the age where they are discovering more about themselves, their interests, their sexuality, and their beliefs. They may not feel comfortable discussing everything with you and prefer to work through their problems alone. All you can do is respect their privacy and be there for them when they need you.

One of the issues that many people face these days is the feeling of loneliness when moving to a new town or city for work purposes. Leaving friends and family behind can make this a very difficult transition as we don't always have the social skills to start making new friends all over again. In the next chapter, I am going to give you some practical advice on how to get to know new people if you are in this situation. as well as strategies for building friendships that will stand the test of time.

New town, new friends, here we come!

Key Points:

- *More and more young people are experiencing loneliness and social isolation today.*

- *Friendships are formed for different reasons, depending on age and abilities.*

- *Young children will often need extra support if they are to be successful at making friends.*

- *Parents can positively contribute to helping their teenage children make friends, even when they are at university.*

HOW TO MAKE FRIENDS IN A NEW CITY

Strangers are just friends waiting to happen – *Rod McKuen*

When I moved from my home town of Manchester to Oxford in 2015, I was ready to take on the world. A few weeks later, I found myself sitting alone in my flat, feeling desperate, homesick, and deflated.

This just wasn't me. I had so many close friends back home and had never felt lonely in my life! I was sociable, outgoing, always being invited to parties, and never had any problems finding people to hang out with. Now, sitting here all alone, I had nobody to talk to and nowhere to go. How could this be happening?

You may have gone through a similar experience of moving to a new town or city for work, only to find yourself friendless in a place where everyone is a stranger. Having to make new friends may have seemed like an impossibility. All of a sudden, you have to handle a new job, new colleagues, a new home, and a new town.

That's a lot for anyone to deal with and can be a very stressful time. As you try to get accustomed to your new circumstances, it's natural to feel a little homesick and you will probably miss your family and friends a lot. After you have managed to settle in and find your bearings, the reality soon sets in that you have no friends in your new town.

The truth is that as you were growing up, you will have formed friendships organically. You may have old school chums, friends from your neighborhood, colleagues who also became your friends, and even your extended family members.

You probably never had to 'try' to make friends because you were always surrounded by people with whom you had forged friendships almost unconsciously over time. Now, you have no idea how to go about making new friends and feel anxious, isolated, and despondent.

That's how I felt at first until I realized that I should be enjoying this new phase of my life instead of wallowing in self-pity. I eventually made a mindset shift and changed my perspective on the situation I found myself in. This was a fresh start for me and I wanted to make the most of it, so I set about making a list of strategies that would enable me to get out more and meet new people.

Once I began implementing my master plan, it became a lot easier to get to know others and it wasn't long before I had met a handful of people who I now call good friends. I'm still connected to my old buddies back home, but I've also got a great support network here now and the experience really helped me to get out of my comfort zone.

You can apply the same strategies if you find yourself in a strange city, and get to meet more people than you probably ever would have back home.

I mention the comfort zone because, under normal circumstances, you don't need to make any effort to find new friends. As a result, you probably haven't developed any social skills that will help you to talk to strangers or develop new relationships from scratch.

When that is the case, it can feel weird or awkward to initiate a conversation with someone you don't know. If you want to enjoy life and feel more fulfilled, you have to put your fears and hesitations to one side. It may sound scary at first, but if you don't give yourself a chance, you'll never know how easy it is.

Social anxiety

It's very common for most people to feel uncomfortable about going out anywhere alone. We tend to crave company for any activity we do and can feel very conspicuous if we have to go somewhere solo. This can be especially true for women, who may also feel vulnerable and fear they are sending out the wrong message.

You probably never had to go anywhere alone, such as a restaurant or theater, as you always had your friends to accompany you. Now, the thought of even walking through your new town alone may make you feel anxious, never mind asking for a table for one at a restaurant.

You could even suffer from physical signs of anxiety such as hot or cold sweats, shortness of breath, palpitations, or worse. This is perfectly normal and there is nothing at all wrong with you. Many people suffer from social anxiety and once you realize that it's a reaction to your fears, you will be able to deal with it more effectively.

Here's the thing: while you are worried about what other people may think on seeing you alone, the likelihood is that they haven't even noticed. If it is obvious that you are alone, they may even admire you for your confidence.

Worrying about what other people think doesn't stop you from excelling in other areas of your life, so why allow it to do so now? In today's society, it's totally acceptable for people to go to a restaurant or cinema alone and even if you are invited to a party, you don't need a chaperone.

It takes time to overcome feelings of social anxiety, but it all begins with how you view yourself. The chances are, other people are far too busy focusing on their own lives to make any judgments about yours. Once you realize that, you can enjoy your time alone stress-free. Be bold and enjoy exploring your new world without worrying about what impression you may be making on others. In reality, you are probably not standing out half as much as you think!

Now, let's take a look at some bulletproof ways to get to know new people. They might start off as complete strangers but could end up becoming your next best friend.

Check your contacts

Before you move to your new location, ask around to see if any of your existing friends or family members know anyone in the town you are moving to. Even if it's an acquaintance who lives there, get their details and be sure to contact them when you arrive.

It could be a relatively distant contact with someone you know from your social media accounts. Simply call or text them and explain you are new to the area. Ask if they can meet up with you over a coffee to give you any tips. That doesn't sound too painful, does it?

Get to know the city

It's a great idea to spend some time getting to know your new town or city. You will probably find tons of information on any local website or at the local tourist information office. Find out more about the history, which neighborhoods sound cool, where the public parks are, or what bars/cafes/restaurants are popular with your age group. Walk around to get a feel for the place, explore, and enjoy discovering something new.

Find out what's going on

No matter how small your new town or community is, there will always be something going on. It could be a local fair or festival, a music performance, a sporting event, or a convention of some kind. Check the local press and follow blogs relating to your new home. Schedule anything that interests you in your calendar and make the effort to attend. You will find plenty of people to mingle with while having fun at the same time.

Take your time

As a newbie in town, you can't expect people to be lining up to get to know you. They may even see you as an outsider at first, and this applies especially in the workplace. Your new colleagues may be too busy to ask you about your background.

They are also likely to already have an established network of friends and don't feel the need to incorporate you in that. It's usually nothing personal – humans generally like to stay with the pack and may be instinctively suspicious of someone they deem as an 'outsider'. Give others the time to get to know you better if you want to see results.

Accept invitations gladly

If your colleagues do ask you out for an after-office drink or a get-together, you may be tempted to turn them down as you feel too shy. This is your opportunity to get to know them better in a more relaxed setting so do take them up on their offer.

It may be the case that they are genuinely keen to learn more about you and you will feel at ease a lot quicker than you imagined. Ask your colleagues if you can connect with them on their social media accounts and start liking their posts. They will love you for that!

Be a conversation starter

If you remember from Chapter 3, I talked in great detail about the art of small talk and ways to start a conversation with someone you don't know or know very little. In the workplace, you may find this a lot easier to do, as you all have something in common. Being the new guy means that you are expected to ask questions, and most people will be very responsive to you.

Apart from talking about work, you can also steer the conversation to more personal things by asking questions like, "What do you all do on the weekends? What's the best place to go clothes shopping around here?" Keep the conversation light and show you are keen to learn more.

Use digital tools

You'll find a lot of apps that have been designed to help people navigate a town or city, offering plenty of info about places of interest, festivals, exhibitions, tours, and so on. Search on TripAdvisor and check out what other users recommend, depending on your interests, and make a note of anything useful. Join platforms that feature get-togethers such as MeetUp.com. The last time I checked it out in

Chapter 2, I found acting courses, meditation workshops, and kayaking weekends going on in my town.

Today, I took another look and found a free Philosophy Seminar, a Sailing Weekend, and a Happy Hour for Entrepreneurs coming up over the next few days. You can also use dating apps if you are looking for a romantic partner but don't forget to make your personal safety the main priority.

Meet a local

It's very popular nowadays to pay for a small personal tour with a local guide. You can book an activity online with platforms such as Lonely Planet or Withlocals and choose from a tour that catches your eye or create a tailor-made day to suit your preferences.

This is a fantastic way to get out, meet someone new, and enjoy a tour of the city. You may be keen to learn about the local cuisine or the architecture of the town, and the cost is relatively small for this kind of activity.

The more you make the effort to get out and about, the more you increase your chances of meeting new people. Staying at home may feel like a safer option but it can very quickly lead to feelings of isolation. This is not good for your emotional wellbeing and although you may enjoy your own company, you also need friends. Once you take that first step, you will realize it's not as difficult as you first thought and your life will be so much richer for it.

You have already taken a giant leap by moving to a different town or city. After overcoming your initial anxiety, you will discover a wonderful new life awaiting you!

Key Points:

- *Making new friends is a social skill we need to practice more.*

- *Social anxiety affects many people but can be overcome.*

- *Change your mindset about going out alone.*

- *Get to know the city and learn where people similar to you hang out.*

- *Connect with your colleagues to make new friends.*

- *Make use of digital platforms and guided tours by locals.*

❧ 10 ❧

HOW TO GET THROUGH THE LONELINESS OF THE HOLIDAY SEASON

C hristmas... is not an external event at all, but a piece of one's home that one carries in one's heart – Freya Stark

For most of us, the holiday season is truly the most wonderful time of the year. Whether it's Christmas, Hanukkah, Thanksgiving, Easter, Ramadan, Diwali, or even New Year, such events are meant to be celebrated with family and loved ones.

Unfortunately, many people have neither, or are living somewhere far away from their nearest and dearest.

They may have recently lost a spouse or partner, gone through a recent break-up, have a social anxiety disorder (SAD), or don't have close relationships with family or friends. For them, the holiday season can be a terribly lonely experience that intensifies feelings of sadness, isolation, and stress.

If you have ever spent an important holiday alone, you will know exactly what I'm talking about. While the rest of the world is enjoying the festivities, you have no one to talk to but yourself or the cat, and that isn't much fun. Often, the build-up to the celebrations is even worse, making you feel anxious just at the thought of it.

While you overhear others talking about their exciting plans for the upcoming occasion, it's easy to feel sorry for yourself and fall into a kind of seasonal depression. You may even feel angry, jealous, or resentful, turning into a miserable grinch for a few days who can't wait until all the festivities are over.

The problem with Christmas

For the purpose of this chapter, I'm going to be talking about being alone at Christmas, although everything you read could also apply to any other day in your festive calendar. The main problem with these big celebrations is that they are highly commercialized and we can't get away from them so easily.

Everyone is expected to be happy, generous, and giving. That sounds great in theory, but if you have no friends or family, it can make you feel as if you are the odd one out. If you don't have any good reason to 'feel happy' on demand, it can all become like some sort of enforced merriment that you don't want to, or can't, participate in.

All of the hype in the weeks leading up to Christmas can also place a lot of financial pressure on many of us and add to our concerns over money problems or debts. We can easily fall into the trap of comparing our lives to others, wishing we had more money, more energy, more family or friends. This sense of lacking in some way is highlighted much more over the holiday season.

There is also a lot of pressure to be sociable at this time of year, with office parties arranged, lavish restaurants booked, and lots of people getting together to be merry. You might find these kinds of gatherings stressful under normal circumstances, and especially at Christmas, where there is an expectation to join in. Intimidating questions like, "What are you doing for Christmas?" loom in the air, leading you to feel awkward if you haven't got anything planned.

Even simple questions such as, "What did you get for Christmas?" can add to the misery when you have no one to give to or receive gifts from.

Occasions like Christmas can quite often be dominated by family conflicts, memories of those you have lost, or a reminder of your loneliness. The stress of that leads many people to think deeply about the negative events in their lives.

The recent COVID-19 pandemic forced most of us into long periods of social distancing, making it impossible to spend time with loved ones. All in all, it really isn't easy to get through any holiday season if you are alone.

Looking at life differently

I think you know by now that this isn't a book about negativity and I'm not going to allow you to feel sorry for yourself, no matter what your circumstances are. You may have very valid reasons for feeling down over the holiday period, and it's not my intention to undermine them. Life is what it is and we all go through difficult times that are often out of our control.

The way we look at life IS in our control though, and it's in our hands to pick ourselves up, switch our mindset, and see things from a different perspective. I know how it feels to be alone at Christmas. One year, I was taking some workshops in Perth, Australia, and had booked a flight to return home to the UK on Christmas Eve.

Unfortunately, it was canceled at the last minute due to bad weather, and I had to spend Christmas Day alone in the airport hotel with only the mini-bar for comfort. All of my plans to spend the holiday with my husband and children were dashed, and I was totally gutted.

It was during that time that I began to think about why we get so stressed out over being alone on days like Christmas. It struck me that we can avoid these intense reactions and cope much better when we become more proactive. Instead of adopting a victim mentality, there are plenty of alternatives that will leave us feeling joyous and content. You don't have to be alone at Christmas and there are ways to spend it with people who might be in exactly the same situation as you.

The three stages of coping

1. Firstly, it's important to look at your mental state and question why you are feeling lonely in the first place. Do you feel like this every day, or just at holiday time? Certainly, if you have been battling loneliness for a while, bringing everything to the surface at Christmas is probably not a good idea.

You need to examine the issue well before that and seek professional help if you suffer from anxiety or depression. Accepting that you are alone is crucial, and deciding to make the most of your day, no matter what, is the right approach to take.

2. Secondly, there are many activities you can get involved in to spend Christmas Day with others. You can offer to do voluntary work, help in a hospice, a retirement home, or a soup kitchen for the homeless. Extra hands are always needed at Christmas as it is the time when charities do a lot of work within the community and any additional help they can get will be much appreciated. It will also give you the opportunity to see that there are many people in a much worse position than you and that you have the capacity to bring them happiness.

3. Thirdly, now is the time to plan ahead for next year to ensure that you won't be alone by then if you would prefer to have company. You can book an off-season vacation, or organize in advance a trip with people who are also likely to be alone this time next year. In the meantime, you have another 12 months to try to improve your social life, make new friends, and patch up any family differences.

The main thing I want to stress here is that you have a choice about how you want to spend Christmas or any major holiday. Grieving, loss, and feelings of sadness are valid emotions, and if you prefer to stay at home by yourself, that is your call. If you find yourself in this situation, learn how to work through your grief and find a place in your heart and mind for acceptance. This will relieve you of a lot of pain and help you to move on. On the other hand, if you feel miserable because you would really prefer to have company, look for ways that you can be part of a communal spirit through volunteering your time to a worthy cause. Here are some practical strategies to help you.

Overcoming loneliness at Christmas

Although everyone around you seems to be caught up in the Christmas hype, you don't have to succumb to the pressure if you don't want to. Relax, take a walk, watch TV, read a book, and simply sail through it doing things you enjoy. That may seem hard to do, but why allow what is going on around you to affect your well-being?

Spoil yourself and do the things that make you feel special, whether that is buying yourself a gift, indulging in your favorite snacks, or spending the day in your pyjamas. Without the pressure to be somewhere else, or cook an enormous lunch for guests, you can savor the time you have to yourself.

Revise your expectations. It's tempting to build your hopes up and believe that you will be able to meet up with friends or family at the last minute. Although that would be nice, it could be a pipedream, so don't bet on it.

Instead, make your own plans for the day and arrange something that will suit you. Buy yourself a nice bottle of wine or schedule a good movie to watch. Don't wait for others to make you feel happy - you can do that very easily by yourself.

Ask around at your local community centers, places of worship, charities, and nonprofit organizations to see if they could use your help on Christmas day.

You will be surprised to find that this is a very gratifying way to celebrate, even with people you have never met before. You could be commandeered to help serve the Christmas lunch or asked to be part of the entertainment. Whatever you do, you certainly won't feel lonely and will forget about your own worries very quickly.

Stay away from social media over the holiday season. Seeing images of party-goers, revelers, and happy families can bring up negative emotions and painful memories.

Even watching Christmas movies can make you feel overwhelmed and if that is the case, opt for something that doesn't revolve around people trying to get home for Christmas.

Check to see if any of your neighbors will also be spending Christmas alone and invite them over for lunch. They may not be able to get out due to a disability, so you could arrange to visit them and even buy a small gift.

After all, Christmas, like many holiday celebrations, is about giving, and that's a feel-good gesture in itself.

Try to plan mentally for the approaching holiday and be prepared to see your emotions or stress intensify as the day looms nearer. Don't leave it until you feel totally wretched and organize something that will prevent you from dwelling on your problems.

Find creative ways to spend your time, such as doing some DIY or going for a long hike.

If you are simply apart from your loved ones, arrange to call them or set a time for a video call. This will help you to overcome your loneliness and you can chat with them for as long as you want to. Call an old friend and catch up with their news. Christmas gives you the perfect opportunity to do this, as it is also a time for reconciliation and well-wishing.

Don't celebrate Christmas at all! It's only one day in the year and by tomorrow, it will be over. I once found myself alone on New Year's Eve and put myself in the mind frame of it being just another day in the week. I bought a big box of chocolates, watched one of my favorite movies, and had a wonderful time!

Help yourself to have a very merry Christmas, despite your current situation, with the above tips. If you still feel it is hard to cope, don't forget that there are many support groups out there to help you. Even talking to a friendly voice at the Samaritans can be extremely beneficial when you are feeling at your lowest and they have trained volunteers to counsel you.

If you are suffering from any kind of social anxiety disorder, contact your mental health services and seek support well before the holiday season arrives.

Take your happiness seriously and don't let anything spoil that. Living a solitary life doesn't have to mean that you suffer. Instead, make the most of your time

alone, get involved in any community activities, and plan for the coming year. Who knows, by that time, you may be surrounded by new friends and creating wonderful memories together.

Key Points:

- *The holiday season can accentuate existing feelings of loneliness and isolation.*

- *Realign your perspectives on being alone and create a new mindset.*

- *Follow the three stages of coping.*

- *Take action to be with others by volunteering your time to a worthy cause.*

- *Overcome feelings of loneliness by applying several of the strategies.*

CONCLUSION

"The most I can do for my friend is simply be his friend." – Henry David Thoreau

Now that we've reached the end of this book, I hope it has given you the courage to go out and make new friends, armed with the knowledge that you need to be able to achieve that.

When I decided to write about this subject, I was moved by the figures coming out from various studies that revealed just how lonely, people were feeling in today's world.

The recent pandemic definitely highlighted or intensified the problem more, with lockdown restrictions and social distancing creating heightened feelings of isolation and stress.

From school-age children and teenagers to millennials and baby boomers, all the evidence to date shows that we are turning into a society of lonely people, which goes against our very nature. We are social beings and need companionship in order to live a healthy life.

Excessive social media use and busy lifestyles are just some of the factors that have contributed to many of us feeling isolated, often lacking the social skills needed to connect with others as much as we would like to.

This book is a positive response to that, and a guide on how to overcome loneliness, no matter what your circumstances are in life.

As we discovered in Chapter 1, having good friends is essential to our mental health, emotional state, and overall well-being. They can even help us to live longer! Nothing can replace having good friends and it's one of the most important relationships we can ever have.

Knowing that so many people find it extremely difficult to forge new friendships is truly heartbreaking and I want to give hope to those of you experiencing that.

A lot of the problem comes down to how to meet new people in the first place and you will have found lots of ideas on how to do that in Chapter 2. Another issue that many of you may struggle with is how to initiate conversations with people you don't know and in Chapter 3 we explored the art of small talk and how to master it.

More often than not, our inability to connect with others stems from our lack of self-knowledge, so Chapter 4 is full of sound advice on how to learn more about yourself and enable people to like you for who you are.

We also looked at how to form long-lasting friendships by nurturing qualities such as empathy and respect in Chapter 5.

In the following chapter, I introduced you to the Pareto Principle, which is an amazing model to apply if you want to focus on deepening your relationships in the most beneficial way. In addition, we delved into the common problem of one-sided friendships, with plenty of tips on how to deal with those successfully.

The last few chapters of the book are dedicated to specific situations where making new friends can be particularly challenging. As a teen or parent, hopefully, you will apply the practical tools you have found here to overcome this problem.

For those of you who feel isolated in a new town or city, or are spending the holiday season alone, I have added lots of useful suggestions that you can adopt to facilitate meeting new people, with advice on how to be more proactive in your life.

In my previous book, **Love Yourself Deeply**, I encouraged you to embrace your inner worth and to feel good about yourself. You are a wonderful person and deserve to be accepted and loved for who you are. By surrounding yourself with good friends who appreciate that fact, it is possible to lead a richer, healthier, and more fulfilled life.

Now that you know how to achieve that, good luck on your friend-making journey!

Whether you are a young adult, a concerned parent, or find yourself alone, use the strategies in this book to help you meet new people, handle the art of small talk, and create meaningful friendships.

Free for you.

10 Weekly Issues of Rebecca's life-changing newsletter "Reclaim Your Power" Rebecca covers Self Love, Self Esteem, Making Friends, Getting Your Life Back & Living A Life of Freedom.

https://rebecca.subscribemenow.com/

Make An Author Happy Today!

I hope you found this book helpful. If you did, I would be eternally grateful if you could spend a couple of minutes writing a review on Amazon.

When you post a review, it makes a huge difference in helping more readers find my book.

Your review would make my day

Thanking you in advance

Rebecca

RESOURCES

Other books by Rebecca

Love Yourself Deeply

The Art of Manifesting Money

How Hard Is It To Make Friends, Patook LLC, 2016

https://patook.com/Blog/MakingFriends

Taylor, M., Carlson, S. M., Maring, B. L., Gerow, L., & Charley, C. M. (2004). The Characteristics and Correlates of Fantasy in School-Age Children: Imaginary Companions, Impersonation, and Social Understanding. *Developmental Psychology, 40*(6), 1173–1187

https://psycnet.apa.org/record/2004-20098-020

Mushtaq, R.Shoib, S.Shah, T.Mushtaq, S.(2014). Relationship Between Loneliness, Psychiatric Disorders and Physical Health? A Review on the Psychological Aspects of Loneliness, 8(9), WE01-WE04 https://jcdr.net/article_fulltext.asp?issn=0973-709x&year=2014&volume=8&issue=9&page=WE01issn=0973-709x&id=4828

The Complete Tales of Winnie-The-Pooh, A.A. Milne, Random House, 1996

Office For National Statistics UK,Children's and young people's experiences of loneliness, 2018

https://www.ons.gov.uk/peoplepopulationandcommunity/wellbeing/articles/childrensandyoungpeoplesexperiencesofloneliness/2018#things-you-need-to-know-about-this-release

Twenge JM, Spitzberg BH, Campbell WK. Less in-person social interaction with peers among U.S. adolescents in the 21st century and links to loneliness. Journal of Social and Personal Relationships. 2019;36(6):1892-1913.

https://doi.org/10.1177%2F0265407519836170

Mental Health of UK Students, Research, Accenture, 2021

https://www.accenture.com/_acnmedia/PDF-158/Accenture-Student-Health-Research-Report.pdf

Made in the USA
Middletown, DE
14 February 2022